Stop the World

Finding a way through the pressures of life

Murray Watts and
Professor Cary L Cooper

Hodder & Stoughton
LONDON SYDNEY AUCKLAND

First published in Great Britain 1998

10 9 8 7 6 5 4 3 2 1

British Library Cataloguing in Publication Data
A record for this book is available from the British Library

ISBN 0 340 67126 2

Typeset by Avon Dataset Ltd, Bidford-on-Avon, Warks

Printed and bound in Great Britain by
Clays Ltd, St Ives plc

Hodder and Stoughton
A division of Hodder Headline PLC
338 Euston Road
London NW1 3BH

Contents

Acknowledgments

The authors and publisher would like to thank the following for their permission to reproduce material in their copyright:

Steve Turner for 'Daily London Recipe' from *Tonight We will Fake Love* (published by Charisma Books); Sheldon Press for the Mother's Stress Checklist from *Coping with Stress: A Woman's Guide* by Dr Georgia Witkin-Lanoil; Michael Joseph for Type A Behaviour from *Type A Behaviour and Your Heart* by M D Friedman & R H Rosenmann; Jonathan Cape for the extract from *Darkness Visible* by William Styron; *The Independent* for the extract from leading articles, September 1991; Macdonald for the extract from *Stress and Relaxation* by Jane Madders; Bloodaxe Books for *No, I'm not Afraid* by Irina Ratushinskaya, translated by David McDuff; McGraw-Hill, Inc. for the table from *Organizational Stress and Preventive Management* by J C Quick & J D Quick (1984); Arrow Books for *Successful Women: Angry Men* by Bebe Campbell-Moore; Faber & Faber Ltd for the quote from 'Four Quartets', *Collected Poems 1909–1962* by T S Eliot. The extract from 'Eleanor Rigby' is © Northern Songs. All rights controlled and administered by MCA Music Ltd under licence from Northern Songs; Kingsway and Monarch Publications for permission to quote from *Rolling in the Aisles* and *Bats in the Belfry* by Murray Watts; and Penguin Books for extracts from *Living with Stress* by Professor Cary L Cooper, Rachel D Cooper and Lynn H Eaker; Columbia Tri-Star International Television for the extract from Steven Zaillian's screenplay of *Awakenings* by Oliver Sacks; Prospect Pictures for material from the BBC series, *Relax*.

Preface

'Stop the world! I want to get off!'

The famous line expresses the secret yearning of millions of people. In recent decades, the well-worn phrase found its way on to T-shirts and postcards and office boards – and it can claim to be one of the most attractive, if impractical, solutions to the pressures of living in the late twentieth century.

In this era of 'hurry-sickness', of rushing around achieving a rise in our blood pressure more surely than a rise in our standard of living, it is impossible to 'stop the world and get off'. But we may be able to do something to change the tempo of our own private world – just enough to take stock of our situation and, if necessary, alter our course with quiet determination.

There are, however, rare occasions in history when the world does seem to stop, when everything comes to a halt and we are compelled to look very carefully at our own lives and at the kind of society we have created. At the time of this book going to press, the nation has been suddenly overwhelmed at the tragic loss of Diana, Princess of Wales. Millions of people are facing questions – for a few brief days at least – which may take many years to work through. Diana is already spoken of as someone who managed to turn the extreme pressures of her own personal and public life into a new kind of fulfilment, a way of being that touched others with its vulnerability and its strength to love against the odds. If this example is her true legacy, it will certainly be a very powerful one. For no one should imagine that finding a way through the pressures of life is an impossibility for them, however difficult their lives, however many mistakes or misfortunes lie in the past. There is always hope, and this seems to be the unexpected message emerging from a period of national grief.

The original version of this book appeared in 1992. It was first published under the title, *Relax: Dealing with Stress*, and accompanied a BBC network series of the same name. We have updated and expanded the book in a number of ways, as well as adding a number of direct quotations from our interviewees for that series. 'Stress' has become a 'buzz word' of our age, and is frequently criticised as simply a catch-all for many complex emotions. Stress, pressure, struggle, the daily battle for survival in life – it doesn't matter what term we choose. We are concerned here with the familiar daily experience of most people, and stress is the word we use in our attempt to describe a tough journey through the pressures of life – which includes looking in detail at the self-destructive patterns of behaviour we can adopt when in trouble. This journey is an individual one, for each reader – and our general emphasis is on this private path, pausing every now and then to gain a wider perspective. Our primary aim has always been to offer hope, and we have expanded the heart of the book here too. Whatever else has changed in recent years, one thing remains the same. The art of survival, in times of great difficulty, involves a belief in the future.

We hope that reading this book will restore and strengthen a belief in your own future.

Murray Watts and Cary Cooper, 8 September 1997

Introduction

Years ago, motorists caught in a tail-back on the M4 motorway would complete their journey into London by filing slowly past a greeting, daubed on a fly-over. Three huge words were splashed in white, one on each arch. The message read simply:
'Good morning lemmings.'

The graffiti has now been scrubbed out and the dry comment on our society long forgotten. However, the self-destructive urge of lemmings to head for the cliff edge is one of nature's dark parables for the human race which will not go away.

Mankind, too, pushes itself to extremes. Forty years of rush-hour madness can be a way of committing slow-motion suicide, ending with death in early retirement. Life lived under the pressure of events at work or in the home can feel like a steep descent into an emotional hell.

This book is for anyone who feels they are heading downwards, towards any kind of precipice. It is for the lemming who would like to be different – and survive.

It is not a book of easy answers but one that aims to be thoroughly realistic. And being realistic means hoping, believing, that change is possible. However, there is one reality we must also face which is that there is no magic pill for a stress-free life. Stress affects us all. It is one of the greatest hazards of twentieth-century life. We may try to live healthy lives, avoiding harmful substances, but it is impossible to avoid stress. We can opt out of plastic bread and nicotine, but not out of bereavements, domestic crises, personality clashes in the office. We only have to walk down a busy road, travel anywhere, to see the impact of stress on our society – the noise, the pollution, the road rage, the insanity of the modern world.

Learning how to deal with stress is increasingly important as a key to our physical survival. It is also the way to improve the quality of our lives, our environment – to make our lives worth living. For many elderly people, increasing longevity simply means greater suffering, more pressure, fear. Knowing how to cope effectively with stress, meeting the challenge of stress and discovering a new peace in ourselves, is the most precious kind of knowledge.

A comic revue on the radio once had an announcement something like this: '*Would Mr David Wilson, of Bexleyheath, please get in touch with himself as he is dangerously ill.*'

That is precisely what we need to do, 'get in touch with ourselves'. If we don't, we become victims of stress and are likely to react in all the wrong ways. Knowing all about stress and, above all, knowing ourselves is an essential requirement for survival – and Part One of the book is devoted to this.

The costs of stress are astronomical. There are economic costs, because of the huge number of working days lost to industry annually through stress-related illnesses (according to the Institute of Management, stress now costs business £7 billion a year), but for many individuals the ultimate price they pay is life itself.

Between 1950 and 1970 the death rate for men aged 34–44, due to coronary heart disease, nearly doubled in England and Wales. By the mid-seventies, heart attacks were far and away the leading cause of male deaths and had increased by 80 per cent over 25 years.

The researches of Friedman and Rosenmann into the link between personality, lifestyle and heart disease, discussed in Part One, graphically illustrate that stress is not a vague problem, something to do with worries and anxieties and our busy schedule: it can be highly specific, as lethal as an arrow aimed by ourselves at our own heart.

'Knowing ourselves' is not some kind of self-indulgence. It can save us from self-indulgence – and self-destruction.

Part Two of the book, 'Victims or Victors?', looks at the way we can adopt 'poor coping strategies'. Given half a chance, many people react to stress by denying it is there, drinking too much, blaming others, or trying desperately to 'work' their way out by becoming a 'workaholic' or obsessively tidy in the home. Part Two, although it looks at negatives, is at least as important as the practical advice given in Part Three. If 'getting in touch with ourselves' is the key, then looking at how we focus on the wrong problems and the wrong solutions is also vital to our survival.

Part Three offers practical suggestions for taking greater control over our lives. It offers some suggestions which, hopefully, may lead to important breakthroughs. No advice can be definitive, nor relevant to all. The economist E F Schumacher wrote a book called *A Guide for the Perplexed*. This book could be called a *Guide for the Distressed*. But it is only a *guide*. Steps can be mapped out, advice given, a friendly hand may steady the journey for some of the way – but making changes is a matter of personal choice.

There are situations, of course, when what we decide has little effect, when our whole environment is so appalling that the odds seem insuperable.

Talking of the effect of stress on premature and low weight births in South Teesside, the consultant obstetrician Dr John Atkins explained:

> 'By stress, I really mean the unopposed or impossible to escape from stress, not the stress when an executive or a prime minister is challenged all the time and can feel they are achieving things. I mean the stress of couples sitting in inadequate homes, in inadequate situations, with inadequate money.'
>
> (*First Tuesday,* ITV, August 1991)

In an area of the country where unemployment was at 33 per cent – three times the national average – at the beginning of the decade, and half of all households lived on less than £100 a week, there was the grim statistic that on average people died ten years younger than their counterparts in the prosperous south of England.

How can any book hope to address such a fundamental level of stress? First of all, there is a special chapter called 'Power and Responsibility' which deals with the much larger issue of corporate and government responsibility for stress in our lives. The overall emphasis of this book is not meant to deny in any way the massive issue of the social and political influences on our existence. However, its main purpose is to concentrate on what we must and can do, whenever possible, ourselves. (For this reason, 'Power and Responsibility' is a separate discussion which can be omitted.)

Even in the worst circumstances which are absolutely beyond our control – as hostage victims have discovered – we must find some way of coping if we are not to be destroyed. We must survive, if we have to, against the odds and when there is no change in our circumstances, even though justice cries out that there must be one day.

Another situation where personal choice can seem very limited is in the case of clinical depression or serious illness, when stress has already taken too heavy a toll. That situation of paralysis is looked at in 'The Stress Equation' at the end of Part One. This book is really aimed earlier down the line. A seriously depressed person will not concentrate enough to read through this book nor see much value in what it has to offer. Negatives will dominate. But in such cases, the book may be valuable to those who are caring and waiting – those who have to believe on behalf of others who have temporarily 'gone down'. Some advice on living with a severely stressed person is given in 'A Problem Shared', at the end of Part Three.

It may be true, as Dr Atkins implied, that executives and politicians can 'feed off' stress. People who believe that they have important decisions to make, sometimes benefit from the challenge of stress. But it is not always so simple:

An eagle once spotted a dead lamb on a block of ice floating

> down a river towards a waterfall. The eagle dived on to the carcass. It fed hungrily, tearing at the meat, knowing that at the last moment it could flap its wings and soar into the heavens. When the floe reached the edge, the eagle flapped its wings powerfully. But it did not move. Its talons had frozen solid on to the ice block.

No one should ever discount the impact of stress on their lives. It can grip slowly or take the unwary by surprise – manifesting itself suddenly in the form of a heart attack or in the traumatic break-up of a marriage.

We all want to enjoy a 'good life', but we all live under stress. We can be immobilised by stress, convinced that nothing will ever alter – but there is always hope. Our decisions and choices have great significance. Nobody could have predicted the sudden collapse of the Iron Curtain, which depended on the choices of many ordinary people, nor the release of Nelson Mandela and the birth of democracy in South Africa. We may not be able to change the world like that, but the extraordinary can happen: barriers can be brought down in our personal experience too, freeing us to live our lives to the full.

Stress, by its very nature, often seems overwhelming but if we are prepared to take it, there is a way through. Someone wrote plaintively, 'I thought I saw light at the end of the tunnel, but it was only some "kind friend" with a torch bringing me more work.' Hopefully, this book will bring genuine illumination, just enough light to keep moving forward. Then, as we travel with determination, the light of our own future will grow much brighter. We will move from wanting to 'stop the world and get off', to wanting quietly to get on – and find a way through.

Part One: Living under Stress

1 What is Stress?

You are trying to meet a deadline. You have one hour to complete a report and catch the post. All day people have been piling into your office and interrupting you. The phones have been going berserk. And now workmen have arrived, as if on cue, to break up the pavement outside. Do you tense up, push your fingers through your hair, chew your pencil, make more typing errors, swear, pace around, glare out of the window in the hope that the workmen will catch your eye? Do you hiss furiously to a colleague: 'I will go crazy if I hear that pneumatic drill one more – just *one more* time!'?

You have money problems. Does the very sight of a brown envelope on your doormat make you feel sick with worry? Do three brown envelopes arriving on the same morning make you feel as if you've been hit by a baseball bat?

Your children have been impossible all day. They have been quarrelling, broken an expensive new toy and pushed a piece of cake into the video recorder. They have redesigned the living room to look as if the Terminator just dropped in for tea. Now you discover that a bar of chocolate has been squashed into the carpet. Do you scream, smash something, sit down and howl? When your partner breezes in from work, blissfully unaware, do you blast him (or her) with accusations: 'You've no idea what my life is like!'? Or do you suppress your feelings, smile lovingly but harbour dark fantasies of revenge?

Your love life is falling apart. You have no job. You can't afford a plumber to fix the leaking cistern in the bathroom. Your cat is ill. Everything seems to be going wrong. Then you get your first job interview in a month. On the day, your heart is racing, your palms sweating as you make your way towards the lift up to the ninth floor. You've never liked lifts. But on the way up you get the worst feeling of panic you've ever had. You feel as if the walls are going to cave in on you. When the secretary meets you at the top, her voice sounds distant. She is saying 'hello', but your throat is too dry to respond. You nod, smile weakly and follow her down interminable corridors. Your prospective employer holds out his hand. He makes a light remark to put you at your ease. You laugh frantically, out of tension. You continue to act nervously throughout the interview, saying with your body language 'I couldn't cope with this job'. When you don't get the job, do you worry whether you'll ever work again? Or worse, do you suffer from endless 'action replays' of your panic in the lift and worry if you'll ever cope with an *interview* again?

You've been through two bereavements in the last year, one of them as the result of a car accident. The telephone rings at 8.30 a.m. Your stomach churns. You think it is bad news. Your heart is pounding as you pick up the receiver, but it is only a friend, apologising for ringing early but she can't make it for coffee until eleven. For an hour afterwards, adrenalin is still pumping into you as images flash through your mind. You live life on the 'edge', week after week, any slight alteration of plans – a son arriving home half-an-hour late from school, a telephone call at an odd hour, events in the world outside, an ambulance siren in the distance, even the theme tune of the regional news report which regularly covers road accidents in the area – all create turmoil in your mind. At the end of a 'bad day', do you feel utterly worn out and constantly on the edge of tears or rage? Do you feel as if no one understands you and no one can help you?

If you have ever experienced anything like the feelings above, you know all about stress. If you ever get 'worked up' about anything, even a trivial matter, stress is taking its toll on you. And if you smoke to calm your nerves or drink too much alcohol to relax, eat compulsively, slim obsessively, have bouts of irrational anger, crying or panic, you are reacting to stress.

No one is free from stress. Our behaviour and our attitudes, even our personalities, can be warped by stress. We can end up believing that the grass is greener everywhere else – if only we could move, change jobs, leave this relationship, quit this marriage, have more money, emigrate. But we cannot escape from ourselves.

Stress is like the bars on our prison. We are trapped in a situation which ruins all quality of life. How do we free ourselves to live again – or love again?

Perhaps we don't feel trapped, but warning lights are beginning to flash in our mind: 'If I don't deal with this situation soon, it'll get worse.' 'What if I get stuck with this feeling of despair?' 'What if my mood never swings back, what if I'm always angry and frustrated like this?' 'What if . . . there's no way out?'

Whatever our situation, if we feel stressed we need to act now. There are many things we can do, but the first step is to understand as clearly as possible what is happening to us. We need to see what causes stress, what are its symptoms and why we get 'worked up'.

Here is a list of some of the typical causes of stress.

Causes of stress

- ***Hurry-sickness*** – madly rushing to meet one deadline after another.
- ***Environmental ill-health*** – poor working conditions, noise, pollution, overcrowded living space.
- ***Caring for others*** – small children, elderly relatives, a sick partner. Having to keep up appearances, feeling exhausted and resentful.
- ***Losing a loved one*** – all kinds of bereavement, including

miscarriage, the death of friends, the death of a pet. Not being able to accept the loss.

- ***Frustrations at work*** – being passed over for promotion, feeling sidelined by changes in the organisation, being understretched, overloaded, working without encouragement or support.
- ***Crisis in work relationships*** – personality clashes, conflicting roles, sexual harassment, favouritism, injustice, group pressure.
- ***Unemployment*** – the shock of being made redundant, loss of self-respect, anxiety about the future, hopelessness after long periods of unemployment.
- ***Boredom*** – feeling listless, frustrated, unfulfilled or apathetic.
- ***Crisis in love relationships*** – unrequited love, infidelity, sexual problems, separation, divorce, loneliness.
- ***Financial worries*** – unpaid debts, unpaid bills, mounting overdraft, low income, collapse of businesses, bankruptcy, repossession of houses.
- ***Fighting on the home front*** – buying, selling and moving house, not being able to move house, being housebound for any reason, facing subsidence, damp, trouble with neighbours, any situation where home ceases to be a haven and becomes a hell.
- ***Family pressures*** – tensions over jobs in the home, sorting out roles in a dual-career partnership, learning difficulties with children, problems with teenagers, having a baby, not being able to have a baby, battles with in-laws, not being able to find time for the marriage.
- ***Fighting bureaucracy*** – dealing with faceless organisations, endlessly being referred to other departments, nothing being done, no one caring.
- ***Illness*** – fear, pain, uncertainty, medical tests. Trying to survive extreme discomfort at home or in hospital. Facing your own or anyone else's death from a terminal illness.
- ***Victims of violence*** – rape, child abuse, incest. Violent death of a relative through accident or murder. Anyone who experiences or lives in fear of mugging, vandalism or burglary. A

traumatic past that continues to disrupt the present and threatens to ruin the future.

- ***Victims of corporate crime or negligence*** – suffering as an innocent investor at the end of a long line of international fraud, feeling helpless in the face of massive irresponsibility. Being involved in a major disaster where no one shoulders the blame and the feelings of injustice add to the shock and bereavement already suffered.
- ***Low self-image*** – not feeling valued, constantly being wounded by others, feelings of rage and powerlessness.

Add your own causes ______________________

____

____

The list of 'stressors' – those things that cause stress in our lives – is potentially a very long one for each of us. Try to be specific in making your own list. What are the major pressure points in your life now? It is important to remember, as you do this, that some things may appear to be the main cause of our stress but in reality they are triggering a much deeper problem.

> Jim can hear the neighbours quarrelling again. Voices are raised, a glass is smashed. Jim is irritated because the noise destroys the calm of his evening watching the snooker. He turns up the volume but the click of snooker balls cannot compete with the terrible row next door. So he switches over to the soccer match on the other side and drowns out what is an irritant to him – but no more. Stephanie, who is also a neighbour, hears the same quarrelling. The shouting and swearing. The same glass being smashed. But the noise means something different to her: the violent argument reminds her of her parents, who fought constantly when she was a little girl. Stephanie is rooted to the spot. She finds herself trembling with fear. No matter how hard she tries to drown the noise with the stereo or the television, the faintest sound

of anger floating through the wall paralyses her. Suddenly, she is a seven-year-old again, gazing through the stair banisters, terrified that her father will kill her mother. The same noise is a nuisance to Jim, but a terror to Stephanie. The fundamental source of her stress lies in her past.

‘I was born without the benefit of family or money or status or anything. I found myself in a home for waifs and strays in the East End of London in the thirties in a slum. I was raised by an old lady called Maw Wren who took in abandoned children; some of them literally left on her doorstep. One of these was wrapped in newspaper – that's why I became a newspaper man, and God help me as I grew up I realised I was totally alone in this world. I've never had the pleasure of meeting my father. I discovered my mother when I was seven or eight: one of the older girls in the home was obviously my mother, and I was raised by Mrs Wren.

My whole life is not dominated by my childhood but haunted by it and I think everything I do has some kind of bearing on what it was like when I was a kid. Take my assessment of people – I can look at someone and in seconds weigh up their character on the basis of whether they are going to be hostile or friendly, cowboys or Indians. You can judge people very quickly. You become very perceptive, very aware, very streetwise and very vulnerable if anyone attacks you. People wonder why I get so upset when I'm monstered by the critics. It really goes back to the childhood, when you're fighting for survival then and someone's attacking you, you're even more in danger. The threat is greater and you kick out, you lash out. You don't know what to do. You're frightened, you're lost and those responses are still there when some toffee-nosed critic in the *Daily Telegraph* has a go at you, nearly sixty years later.’

(Derek Jamieson, journalist and broadcaster, from the TV series, *Relax*, BBC/Prospect Pictures, 1992)

Defining stress

What exactly is stress? There are many different definitions:

- Stress is getting worked up.
- Stress is feeling we can't cope.
- Stress is being trapped in a situation we can't change.
- Stress is fighting a losing battle to gain control.
- Stress is when both body and mind are hurting because we are under too much pressure.

One very simple definition of stress is that: stress is a four-letter word – 'pain'.

Stress, according to psychology professor Richard Lazarus, is experienced when 'there are demands on a person which tax or exceed his adjustive resources'. We can't handle a situation because it is getting 'too much'. We haven't got the strength or the will to go on – but we go on anyway and the effort costs us dearly. Another explanation is that stress arises from 'negative thoughts about our environment'.

'I am having to face a situation I don't like.'

'I don't think I can cope.'

We experience stress when we have doubts about coping. Certainly, we are at our most stressed when the struggle to adapt to circumstances gets on top of us. We feel we can't carry on. Everything seems a struggle. We can imagine our epitaph: 'Here lies a person who fought the good fight – and lost!'

Stress and the body

It's no coincidence that we often speak of our lives as a struggle or a fight. We 'battle through'. We feel defeated and wish we could run away. All these emotions are part of our ancient inheritance as human beings, our animal identity. The reactions of 'fight or flight' are instinctive ways of behaving under threat.

Let's imagine our ancestor, Urgg, climbing over a boulder. Suddenly he is confronted by Thwakk, who is wielding a huge club. He has a split-second choice to fight or to run for it. Urgg is smaller than Thwakk and sensible. He runs for it. Finally he escapes. He lies panting in his cave. Gradually his body returns to its normal level of calm. All is well. But suppose Thwakk had chased him for miles and miles. Urgg might well collapse from exhaustion and even die. His body would be keyed up for too long and be pushed beyond the limits of its resources. He would 'burn out'.

Hans Selye, the physician and scholar, described this pattern as the General Adaptation Syndrome. According to him, coping with a crisis or threat has three stages:

1. Initial alarm or surprise leading to fight or flight.
2. The resistance stage. The body keys up to cope with the crisis and then returns to normal.
3. Exhaustion. If the state of alarm or the fight–flight reaction continues over too long a period, reserves will be burnt up. Any creature unable to alter its behaviour successfully will eventually die.

Karl Albrecht, in his book *Stress and the Manager*, describes how stress causes the body to 'rev up' for action. 'Fight or flight' stress chemicals are released into the body. The hypothalamus in the brain triggers the pituitary gland. Hormones are released which activate the adrenal glands, immediately increasing the output of adrenalin into our bloodstream. We can feel our 'stomach churning'. The adrenalin, along with corticosteroid hormones, dramatically ups our level of arousal:

- Blood supply to the brain is increased, improving our judgement.
- Our heart speeds up, pumping more blood to our muscles, and our breathing rate improves.
- Glucose and fats are released into the bloodstream, giving us extra energy.
- Blood is drained from the stomach, intestines and skin (giving us cold hands and feet) to be used efficiently elsewhere.

All these changes are controlled by the sympathetic branch of our nervous system. The parasympathetic has the opposite function. It helps us to relax, to sleep. It produces feelings of tranquillity, as well as controlling our reproductive system.

When stress chemicals build up in our bodies, when we get 'worked up' and 'psyched up' for action, but do not act – we do not fight or run for it but simply and literally 'stew in our own juice' – then the problems come. Stress researchers believe that continual states of anxiety and tension which are not 'worked through' lead to physical as well as emotional ill health.

Civilisation does not allow us to deal with stress by lifting up our word processor and smashing it down on the skull of an awkward colleague, or running screaming down the street every time we have a domestic problem. There is no primitive solution, no easy escape and no way to stop the world and get off. Most of us have to face the same situations, day in, day out, the same family, the same colleagues, the same environment, the same pressures, and the same building up of stress – and the same inability to deal with it.

Symptoms of stress

We have looked at definitions of stress. We can add another – stress is the opposite of being relaxed. It's 'getting uptight'. The language we apply to the stressed person is revealing: 'knotted up', 'keyed up', 'twisted up', 'hyped up', 'holding themselves in'. Relaxation is the opposite. It's all about 'letting go'. Some of the advice people give to those under pressure is equally telling:

'Hold on tight!'
'Hang on in there!'
'Chin up!'
'Pull yourself together!'
'Keep a stiff upper lip!'
'Get a grip on yourself!'
'Don't lose your head!'

As if these contortions were not difficult enough, the poor victim of stress is then told:

'Don't panic!'

'Keep smiling!'

No wonder life becomes an immense effort when we are dealing with stress. Physically, it's like being in a wrestling ring. Emotionally, it's like being on stage. Smiling, waving, the show must go on.

But even if we hide the truth of how we are feeling, it leaks out in other ways. The stress in our lives becomes obvious – to others at least – in so many ways. Our tics and twitching, our knee-hugging, our hair-twirling, our biro-sucking, our foibles and jerky speech patterns, our mood swings, all give us away. Our slow, painstaking destruction of a polystyrene cup in a stressful board-meeting reveals more than the minutes will ever record.

Check yourself against the list of well-known symptoms of stress on the next page.

1. Physical Symptoms of Stress	***2. Behavioural Symptoms of Stress***	***3. Some Physical and Mental Conditions Associated with Stress***
Lack of appetite	Constant irritability with people	Asthma
Craving for food when under pressure	Feeling unable to cope	Colitis
Frequent indigestion or heartburn	Lack of interest in life	Rheumatoid arthritis
Constipation or diarrhoea	Constant, or recurrent, fear of disease	Peptic ulcers
Insomnia	Difficulty in making decisions	Skin disorders
Constant tiredness	Nail biting	Depression
Tendency to sweat for no good reason	Loss of interest in other people	M.E.
Nervous twitches	Suppressed anger	Hypertension: high blood pressure
Headaches	A feeling of being the target of other people's animosity	Coronary thrombosis: heart attack
Cramps and muscle spasms	Loss of sense of humour	
Nausea	Feeling of neglect	
Breathlessness without exertion	Frequent crying or desire to cry	
Fainting spells	Dread of the future	
Impotency or frigidity	A feeling of having failed as a person or parent	
	Difficulty in concentrating	
	The inability to finish one task before rushing on to the next	
	Fear of being alone	
	Inability to sit still without fidgeting	

Stress, if handled wrongly, affects us physically and emotionally. Physically, it winds us up. We need to unwind. We need to relax. Emotionally, it makes us uptight. We need to let go of our problems and, in letting go, we can take back control of our lives.

The exercises in the third part of this book are aimed at encouraging this process – but equipping ourselves mentally for the journey to a healthier life begins now. We need to investigate some of the deeper underlying factors in stress.

Change

Our failure to adjust to change is one of the greatest causes of stress in our lives.

A close relative dies. We cannot accept the loss. Our situation has changed but we cannot adjust. We cannot live life as it is *now*. We lose our job, we retire, we marry, divorce, give birth, move house, get promoted, demoted, fall in love, get jilted, make money, plunge into debt: change. Everywhere, in almost every experience, there is change.

The stationmaster's cry 'All change, please!' means getting off the train at the end of the line on to another that is going somewhere. But we don't find it easy to do that. Sometimes we sit on the old empty train of our lives and pretend that it's moving. We don't like change.

Quite apart from the ups and downs of experience, life takes us through many changes which are to do with our age and role in life. We cannot avoid growing up and growing old – and we cannot avoid deep changes in our lives. We have to adjust, sometimes very painfully – whether it's to going to school, leaving home, turning forty or going through the menopause.

Seven Ages of Stress

Shakespeare spoke of 'seven ages of man' in our journey from the cradle to the grave. We can borrow his idea and look at the 'seven ages of stress':

1 Joe is three weeks old. To his parents' despair, he cries all through the night. Since leaving the security of the womb, he has been in an incubator, a hospital cot, a carry cot in the car, and now he has come home to a new cot, a new bedroom and a hoard of relatives peering down at him. There is so much change in his little life that he is struggling to adjust and given half a chance, he would prefer to return to the womb.

2 Andrew is five years old and he has spent his first few weeks at school. He is anxious in the mornings, complaining of tummy upsets. Some days he wets himself at school. He is fractious and disobedient when he comes home. He is suffering the stress of a major readjustment.

3 Katie is fifteen. She panics when a boy she fancies rings up. She goes hot and cold at the sound of his voice. She is elated when he calls round. She feels like killing herself when he decides to go out with her best friend. She gets depressed and irritable. She is petrified of failing her exams. She secretly fears she may be adopted. She is sure her parents are going to divorce. Worry gives her headaches. She is afraid she has a brain tumour. Katie is a perfectly ordinary teenager going through one of the most stressful transitions in human life: she is changing from a child into an adult.

4 Sue is twenty. She is an extremely calm and able student nurse, facing her finals for her RGN. She has gone through very demanding changes in the last three years, including living a hundred miles from family and friends, feeling lonely and coping with the ups and downs of her social life. She suffers from migraines, particularly when she has time off to relax. For many months, she has been working varying shifts and changing wards every nine weeks, with a report on each ward which is crucial to her result. She is exhausted and lives in fear of making an error which would not only mean failure to graduate but could mean prosecution. As well as migraines, she is suffering from

disrupted sleep, nightmares and bouts of depression – although outwardly she is successful and popular with her patients. Sue is adjusting to the massive changes required by her first job, but at considerable cost to her peace of mind.

5 Ben is thirty. He is married and doing very well in his business. His wife, Jill, has been pursuing a successful career too – but she has just had a baby. Ben is trying to share the responsibility but deep down he feels that Jill should not go back to work. There is tension between them. Neither Ben nor Jill realised that having a baby was a much bigger adjustment than getting married. Their relationship is changing. Jill is committed to her career but feels torn by her new responsibilities and decides not to return to work for two years. Ben feels that this temporary compromise is fair but Jill is not so sure. Her feelings are complex and confused. She has adjusted to suit her husband but the stressful situation has not been avoided. It has been buried inside her. Meanwhile, Ben is reacting to tension in the home by working extremely late in the office and by drinking too much. He is altering his behaviour, but not in a way that will help himself or his family.

6 Pauline is fifty. She has been divorced for ten years and has brought up two children on her own. She has survived the traumatic break-up of her marriage well, but now she is adjusting to two mid-life challenges: menopause, and both her children leaving home to go to college. The divorce hits her afresh. She is suddenly alone after investing years of her emotional life in her children. A breast cancer operation, although successful, causes further shock and readjustment. Pauline is determined to beat this threat and survive – she always has done – but life seems to be piling up the odds against her. She has lost her part-time job and cannot find further work. Both her children are struggling themselves, emotionally and financially, and need her full support. The changes in their lives make it much harder for her to cope with the problems on her own.

7 Arthur is seventy-five. He was a pit-deputy at the local colliery when it was at the height of its productivity. Now the mine has closed, a derelict ruin – which seems like a symbol of the changes in Arthur's life. He was once tall and athletic. Now he is stooping and arthritic. He was once the most popular regular at the local pub. Now he is too frail to go out, and if he did, he might fall victim to muggers. Urban planning, recession and violence have changed the world of his youth from a close-knit community into a concrete wilderness. Yet, even with all these changes, Arthur was coping very well – until his wife died. This was one change too many. He finds it impossible to adjust. At the moment, he sees no life or future without her and constantly talks of his own death. His grandchildren, who love him, are beginning to tire of visiting him because they cannot cope with his gloominess – nor can they understand what it is like to go through so many desperately painful changes.

It is not only the well-known life changes, but all the little changes, the slow and the sudden twists of experience, which cause stress. And change not only affects each individual life profoundly, but also affects businesses and corporations. The management expert Peter F Drucker takes the view that it is essential for management to anticipate change. Successful businesses 'see change as normal, even healthy'. Change, in his view, needs to be regarded not as a threat but as an opportunity.

It is not easy to translate such a positive attitude into personal terms but it is true to say that *the amount of stress we experience in life is directly related to our ability to adjust to change.*

Control

A line from a Bob Dylan song runs: '*Something is happening but you don't know what it is, do you, Mr Jones?*'

When we don't understand what's going on, we feel trapped.

When change is rapid and overwhelming, as it has been throughout this century, we feel confused and powerless. Huge sprawling cities, traffic pollution, crime, population explosion, the greenhouse effect. What can we do about this? What can we do about all the bad news on television? AIDS? Vandalism? The fact that car thefts have risen by 65 per cent in one year in our area? That fifteen-year-olds have 'ram-raided' a jeweller's shop down the street for the third month running, that dogs are barking, radios blaring, the streets are unsafe? What can we do?

It is significant that neighbours' barking dogs, heavy traffic noise and dealing with large bureaucracies came top of a recent survey of stressful experiences. They are all situations over which we feel we have little or no control. We could add our home situations and work environments too, because so often we feel we have no control and no power to change anything.

The amount of stress we experience is directly related to how much control we have – or feel *we have – over events.*

> 'It's the things I can't control that get me worked up more than anything else, even though I know it's totally irrational and unreasonable. Like once we were doing a *Kilroy* in the Costa and we'd all arrived there with beautiful blue skies. And the day we're going to do the show it's threatening to rain and the wind is blowing and everybody's saying we've got to cancel the show. Now that really got me stressed more than anything else. It's the one thing I can't do anything about. The fact that on this occasion I might have my wife saying, "Don't be silly, you can't do anything about it so you might as well forget about it and go", doesn't help. That just makes it worse. That compounds the aggravation, because Yes, of course I know I can't change the weather. I don't need to be told that I can't change the weather.'
>
> (Robert Kilroy-Silk, broadcaster, from the TV series, *Relax*, BBC/Prospect Pictures, 1992)

Life experience

Our perceptions vary so much according to our personalities and our experience of life. Some people feel they have no control when they do have some. Others believe that there is always something they can do even when it's against the odds. Some react much more strongly to a smaller problem than a larger one. In the illustration earlier in this chapter, Stephanie overreacted to the noise of an argument – but she may well handle a redundancy better than Jim, who might be totally unable to cope with such a shock. It all depends on our background, our temperament and our experience of life.

In the 1960s, two researchers, Thomas Holmes and Richard Rahe, developed a 'life-events scale' which charts how events in our lives ranging from bereavement to moving house, from marriage to money problems, from good to bad experiences of changing circumstances, can affect our health. The original 'life-events scale', though, does not allow for our own perception of events. How we see what happens to us in life is a critical factor in the level of stress we experience. (Hence the scale of 1–10 that follows.)

The following chart, which was designed by Cary and Rachel Cooper for a study on breast cancer, will help you to assess your stress level in coming to terms with recent events in your life.

Life events

Place a cross (X) in the 'Yes' column for each event which has taken place in the last two years. Then circle a number on the scale which best describes how upsetting the event crossed was to you, e.g. 10 for death of husband.

Event	*Yes*	*Scale*
Bought house		1 2 3 4 5 6 7 8 9 10
Sold house		1 2 3 4 5 6 7 8 9 10
Moved house		1 2 3 4 5 6 7 8 9 10
Major house renovation		1 2 3 4 5 6 7 8 9 10
Separation from loved one		1 2 3 4 5 6 7 8 9 10

Event	Yes	Scale
End of relationship		1 2 3 4 5 6 7 8 9 10
Got engaged		1 2 3 4 5 6 7 8 9 10
Got married		1 2 3 4 5 6 7 8 9 10
Marital problem		1 2 3 4 5 6 7 8 9 10
Awaiting divorce		1 2 3 4 5 6 7 8 9 10
Divorce		1 2 3 4 5 6 7 8 9 10
Child started school/ nursery		1 2 3 4 5 6 7 8 9 10
Increased nursing responsibilities for elderly or sick person		1 2 3 4 5 6 7 8 9 10
Problems with relatives		1 2 3 4 5 6 7 8 9 10
Problems with friends/ neighbours		1 2 3 4 5 6 7 8 9 10
Pet-related problems		1 2 3 4 5 6 7 8 9 10
Work-related problems		1 2 3 4 5 6 7 8 9 10
Change in nature of work		1 2 3 4 5 6 7 8 9 10
Threat of redundancy		1 2 3 4 5 6 7 8 9 10
Changed job		1 2 3 4 5 6 7 8 9 10
Made redundant		1 2 3 4 5 6 7 8 9 10
Unemployed		1 2 3 4 5 6 7 8 9 10
Retired		1 2 3 4 5 6 7 8 9 10
Increased or new bank loan/mortgage		1 2 3 4 5 6 7 8 9 10
Financial difficulty		1 2 3 4 5 6 7 8 9 10
Insurance problem		1 2 3 4 5 6 7 8 9 10
Legal problem		1 2 3 4 5 6 7 8 9 10
Emotional or physical illness of close family or relative		1 2 3 4 5 6 7 8 9 10
Serious illness of close family or relative requiring hospitalisation		1 2 3 4 5 6 7 8 9 10
Surgical operation experienced by family member or		

Event	***Yes***	***Scale***
relative		1 2 3 4 5 6 7 8 9 10
Death of husband/wife		1 2 3 4 5 6 7 8 9 10
Death of family member or relative		1 2 3 4 5 6 7 8 9 10
Death of close friend		1 2 3 4 5 6 7 8 9 10
Emotional or physical illness of yourself		1 2 3 4 5 6 7 8 9 10
Serious illness requiring your own hospitalisation		1 2 3 4 5 6 7 8 9 10
Surgical operation on yourself		1 2 3 4 5 6 7 8 9 10
Pregnancy		1 2 3 4 5 6 7 8 9 10
Birth of baby		1 2 3 4 5 6 7 8 9 10
Birth of grandchild		1 2 3 4 5 6 7 8 9 10
Family member left home		1 2 3 4 5 6 7 8 9 10
Difficult relationship with children		1 2 3 4 5 6 7 8 9 10
Difficult relationship with parents		1 2 3 4 5 6 7 8 9 10

Plot your total score.

Stress score

1–25	26–50	51–75	75–100
Low	Moderate	Medium	High

Many of the events listed above would merit a book to themselves. For example, there are so many different types of bereavement and degrees of loss. It is impossible to simply talk of 'bereavement'. Our experience could be:

- Death of a loved one after a long, painful illness – deep sadness tinged with some relief.
- Death of a partner in an unhappy marriage – unresolved feelings of guilt and anguish.

- Sudden death of a close relative or friend from a heart attack – shock as well as grief.
- Violent death of a child – extreme shock, grief, anger, perhaps leading to 'post traumatic stress disorder'.
- Loss of a pet that has been a companion to a lonely person – a grief hard to explain or share, increasing isolation.

It is easy to be glib and say to those suffering 'I know how you feel'. We rarely do. But we can look closely at ourselves. *The more important and painful an event is – in our own estimation – the greater the effort we need to adjust and the more stress we experience.*

Too high a score on the life-events scale frequently leads to physical or mental ill-health. We need to look carefully at what is happening in our lives and take good care of ourselves. It may not be right to move house, change job and have a baby in a year of bereavement and family illness. We may have no options, but there is often something we can do to affect the pattern of our lives. ('Life-planning' is discussed in Part Three.)

Lifestyle

It's not only what happens in life – but the way we live life that produces stress. Poor diet, lack of fitness and leisure time, over-indulging ourselves, smoking, drinking too much, endless rush. Much of our behaviour is to blame for the stress in our lives. In fact, lifestyle may be the major factor, the very thing we need to adjust urgently in order to cope successfully with the other stresses which we cannot avoid.

But it's not just us. The world is to blame too. Our so-called civilisation creates a lot of stress, twisting our lives out of shape. Steve Turner's poem (on the next page) about the London rush hour says it all.

Daily London Recipe

Take any number of them
you can think of,
pour into empty red bus
                    until full,
and then push in
                    ten more.
Allow enough time
to get hot under the collar
before transferring into
multistory building.
Leave for eight hours,
and pour back into same bus
                    already half full.
                    Scrape remainder off.
When settled down
tip into terraced houses each
carefully lined with copy
of *Evening Standard* and *Tit Bits*.
Place mixture before open
television screen at 7 p.m.
and then allow to cool
in bed at 10.30 p.m.
May be served with
working overalls
or pinstripe suit.

(Steve Turner, from *Tonight We Will Fake Love*)

Disappointment

It could be said that growing up begins with our first disappointment. The birthday present that wasn't what we wanted, the Christmas when Santa failed to deliver, the day our prayer wasn't answered, the time our parents let us down or the realisation that first love was only first lust. Shattered expectations are one of the greatest causes of stress. And it goes on happening through the years. We are constantly vulnerable to disappointment because we idealise and fantasise about life – and we are encouraged to do this.

We live in a society where we prepare for weddings but not marriage, birth but not motherhood. We anticipate these events for months and spend large sums of money preparing for the 'great day', for the 'happy news'. But we spend only a fraction of this time preparing for reality.

One of the most agonising examples of defeated expectations has been the 'boom-bust' cycle of recent decades. A report, 'Self-employment in the UK', from the Institute of Manpower Studies at Sussex University, shows that between June 1978 and June 1989 the number of self-employed people rose from 1.84 million to 3.10 million. Some of these people were choosing self-employment as if it were a ride on the gravy train of the enterprise culture – but the harsh reality in the nineties was very different. In the first six months of 1991, 13,000 businesses failed and in 1992 nearly 100 small businesses were failing every day. Behind many such statistics is a broken dream, the stress of a vision that has faded, of an identity and future in question, as well as the massive pressure of financial losses. (For an examination of our increasingly 'freelance culture', see the chapter, 'Power and Responsibility'.)

In recent years, it is significant that investment schemes have been compelled by law to carry the rider: 'Remember that the value of shares can go down as well as up.' Failure to recognise this painful truth about our life experience in general – marriage, family, career – can lead to disillusionment and despair, a hopelessness that can delay recovery and limit the 'bounce-back' factor that we need for survival.

Work stress

This brings us to the subject of stress produced by our work – or lack of it. Work stress takes many forms, from impossible deadlines to noisy and filthy working conditions, to individual problems like sexual harassment. Whatever their circumstances, the vast majority of people suffer daily from work stress. For example:

- The employee who enjoys work but comes under pressure from above.
  ('My boss makes unreasonable demands.')
- The employee who is frustrated by the very nature of the job.
  ('If only I could move to another firm.')
- The insecure freelancer.
  ('Where's the next job coming from?')
- The temporarily unemployed.
  ('I may never work again.')
- The long-term unemployed.
  ('I know I'll never work again – there's no future for me.')

Some work stress 'comes with the job'. Few of us envy the life of the traffic warden or the bomb disposal expert. But the stresses we face may be just as severe.

One television executive was heard to say, during a recent shake-up in his company, 'Things have got so bad now, people are stabbing each other in the chest.'

Stress can have a domino effect in a large corporation. An executive threatened with redundancy commented: 'The trouble is, the very people who are trying to reassure me are in danger of losing their own jobs.' Stress is infectious. Problems in the industry mean problems for the individual. The culprit is not always 'recession', either. Bad management can leak down through the system affecting everyone. No one is secure. The work environment is charged with anxiety in such a situation.

Then there is the problem of overload. Perhaps this is the most widely recognised agent of stress. When we have too much to do, in too little time, without enough back-up, we become liable to explosions of anger, ill-health, domestic problems, sleeplessness. We also make errors of judgement. American GIs, arriving in Vietnam, were often so stressed during early operations that they would open fire on monkeys in the forest. Errors, confusion, chaos – 'overload'. This experience, which can lead to 'burn-out' in a professional context, was vividly described by one school teacher in a comprehensive school:

> 'I have feelings of not achieving anything: it is pointless; I have feelings of depression; I have tension in my head; I have lost half a stone in three months; I switch from one decision to another – I will leave – No, I won't; cannot switch my mind off; feelings of panic; I can't watch television; I thought I was going crazy; disturbed sleep and eating; I stopped going to meetings; I can't face going to school.'
>
> (Quoted in *Stress in Teaching* by Jack Dunham)

When we experience such an extreme level of work stress, it's as if all the alarm bells are ringing, sirens are sounding in our head. If we were machines (and we're not – this is our problem) then a red light would be flashing 'RED ALERT! RED ALERT! OVERLOAD! OVERLOAD!'

However, there is an opposite problem which we are far less aware of, but which is equally serious. When we are under-used at work, not stretched or challenged at all, or suffering from the chronic boredom of a monotonous task or, worse, the desert landscape of unemployment when days merge into nights, weeks, years of aimlessness, then deep inside – unnoticed – another red light is flashing 'UNDERLOAD! UNDERLOAD!'

Experiments have shown that a person, submerged in a tank of water in darkness, with no stimulus of light, sound, touch, or taste, after a brief period of calm will very soon become highly stressed. Such a situation can only be endured for about eight hours – but some people are perilously 'under-loaded' for years.

John Ruskin put the matter very plainly nearly 150 years ago:

'In order that people may be happy in their work, these three things are needed: they must be fit for it; they must not do too much of it; and they must have a sense of success in it.'

If your work experience is one of the principal causes of stress in your life, then complete the following questionnaire:

Measure Your Own Daily Stress at Work

Circle the number that best reflects the degree to which the particular statement is a source of stress for you at work.

	Rarely or never stressful		*Stressful*		*A great deal of stress*	
Trouble with client/customer	0	1	2	3	4	5
Having to work late	0	1	2	3	4	5
Constant people interruptions	0	1	2	3	4	5
Trouble with boss	0	1	2	3	4	5
Deadlines and time pressures	0	1	2	3	4	5
Dealing with the bureaucracy at work	0	1	2	3	4	5
Technological breakdowns (e.g. computer)	0	1	2	3	4	5
Trouble with work colleagues	0	1	2	3	4	5
Too many jobs to do at once	0	1	2	3	4	5
Telephone interruptions	0	1	2	3	4	5
Travelling to and from work	0	1	2	3	4	5
Travelling associated with job	0	1	2	3	4	5
Making mistakes	0	1	2	3	4	5
Job interfering with home/ family life	0	1	2	3	4	5
Can't cope with in tray	0	1	2	3	4	5
Can't say 'no' when I should	0	1	2	3	4	5
Not enough stimulating things to do	0	1	2	3	4	5
Too many meetings	0	1	2	3	4	5

	Rarely or never stressful		***Stressful***		***A great deal of stress***	
Having to tell colleagues or subordinates unpleasant things	0	1	2	3	4	5
Co-ordinating activities with colleagues or boss	0	1	2	3	4	5

Total all your scores. The following is a rough guide to your stress level at work:

80–100 You are experiencing a great deal of stress in many aspects of your job. Seek help

50–79 You are currently experiencing a moderate amount of stress at work, in some but not all aspects of your job

20–49 There are some pressure points at work but not all-encompassing

0–19 You are reasonably satisfied at work, with few if any pressures

No matter what your total score is, if you score 4 or 5 on any particular item, it is a problem which you will probably need to deal with.

(Cartwright, S and Cooper, C L (1997), *Managing Workplace Stress*, London: Sage Publications)

Mother's stress

No woman with children needs reminding that motherhood is the most gruelling and demanding – unpaid! – profession in the world.

> 'For mothers nowadays, there is an enormous amount of stress because of their own high expectations and the high expectations of society. Generally, I think, people are more aware of a connection between childhood experience and adult life and many mothers want to get this right. I write regularly for a weekly magazine where I answer parents' letters so I know from that that so many women want to do things right with their child but there is no way you can do things perfectly. A friend once told me that the most comforting thing I ever said to her was a mother's place is in the wrong. You see, you've got to get it wrong, otherwise your child will never want to separate from you and grow up. But which bits of

getting wrong will be okay and which bits will cause enormous problems, we don't know. And this isn't explained to mothers any more than the ordinary everyday problems of babies that cry. Mothers get lots of good training in giving birth but they don't get any training in what happens in the weeks after that. And that's when nobody's interested, nobody comes round to say, "You're doing fine, this is what babies do", which is all that you want to hear over those weeks. Society is very critical of this. If a child misbehaves in public, the mother is blamed. Rather than people helping her, they blame her. So I think the young mother is one of the most difficult and least appreciated jobs in society today.'

(Dorothy Rowe, psychologist, from the TV series, *Relax*, BBC/Prospect Pictures, 1992)

The Mother's Stress Checklist, devised by Dr Georgia Witkin-Lanoil (*Coping with Stress: A Woman's Guide*), is an extremely revealing 'alternative' work stress guide.

Mother's Stress Checklist

Nine-to-five hours? Call in for a sick day? Maternity leave from maternity? Not a chance! High risk for the female stress syndrome? Without a doubt!

If you are a mother, fill out this mother's stress checklist and see how high a risk you're running. To the left of each item, write your points according to the following scale:

0 NEVER TRUE
1 RARELY TRUE
2 SOMETIMES TRUE
3 FREQUENTLY TRUE
4 ALWAYS TRUE

Activities

I can completely lose interest in social activities and hobbies; the effort seems too great. ☐

I find it difficult to know what I would like to do with free time. ☐

I forget what chore I have started and don't follow through with plans. ☐

I start more projects than I can possibly finish. ☐

I feel the house must be spotless and run with complete efficiency. ☐

I find myself feeling overwhelmed and out of control because there are too many demands on me. ☐

I find it hard to say no to my children or husband, even when I think I am right to say no. ☐

Self-concept

I feel that my appearance doesn't really matter to me or anyone else. ☐

I feel that there is very little time for me in my day. ☐

I think other people's opinions are more valid than mine. ☐

I feel unappreciated by my family. ☐

I fantasise about what my life would be like if I could start again. ☐

I find I exaggerate and boast to friends. ☐

I feel a sense of resentment and anger that I cannot really explain. ☐

I find that I often look for compliments and praise. ☐

Appetite

I feel too aggravated or tense to eat. ☐

I crave coffee or cigarettes to keep me going. ☐

I binge and then regret it. ☐

I need chocolate and/or other carbohydrates when I feel tired or down. ☐

I suffer from nausea, cramps, or diarrhoea. ☐

I snack too often. ☐

Sleep

I have trouble falling asleep. ☐

I awaken earlier than I need/want to. ☐

I have nightmares. ☐

I do not feel rested even when I have a full night's sleep. ☐

I fall asleep earlier than I want to in the evening. ☐

I seem to need a nap in the afternoon. ☐

I awaken during the night. ☐

Outlook

I feel like I've lost my sense of humour. ☐

I feel impatient and irritable. ☐

I cry without knowing why. ☐

I relive the past. ☐

I am pessimistic about the future. ☐

I feel numb and emotionless.

I feel myself laughing nervously, too loudly, or without reason. ☐

I ignore things that would upset me. ☐

I am sorry that I chose motherhood. ☐

TOTAL ___

As with the Work Stress questionnaire, this checklist may be useful in indicating particular areas of stress for you, rather than working out totals. However, with a maximum of 148, any figure of around 70 upwards is an undesirable level.

2 Knowing Ourselves

When Alice finds herself in Wonderland, everything starts to change so rapidly she doesn't know where or who she is any more:

> 'Let me think: was I the same when I got up this morning? I almost think I can remember feeling a little different. But if I'm not the same, the next question is, "Who in the world am I?" Ah, that's the great puzzle.'

When we are confused by events and feeling stressed, we may well ask: 'Who am I? Where do I fit in?' Sometimes we have a very good idea exactly where we fit 'in the order of things' – but we don't like the result. Joe Lampton, in *Room at the Top* by John Braine, begins to hate himself. His climb to the top has cost him his true identity:

> 'I didn't like Joe Lampton. He was a sensible young accountant with a neatly pressed suit and a stiff white collar. He always said and did the right thing and never embarrassed anyone with an unseemly display of emotion . . . I hated Joe Lampton, but he looked and sounded very sure of himself, sitting at my desk in my skin; he'd come to stay, this was no flying visit.'

Sometimes we recognise all too well what we have become. Yet we still don't know who we really are. Can we find ourselves again or are we lost? Have the pressures of life squeezed us into the wrong shape for ever?

'It's easy to blame other people when things go wrong in our lives, but often the real truth is that we're angry at ourselves and at our own inability to cope. To get back our self-confidence we need to regain control. Sometimes it's necessary to stop and take stock. Given the hectic place at which most of us live our lives, finding time to pause and take stock is a luxury we tend to deny ourselves. Often something drastic has to happen before we really think about what we're doing with our lives or what we would like to be doing.'

(Martyn Lewis, newscaster, from the TV series, *Relax*, BBC/Prospect Pictures, 1992)

The perfect fit

One definition of peace is a 'perfect fit' between ourselves and our environment – knowing *who* we are and liking *where* we are and feeling a profound sense of belonging, a harmony between ourselves and the world: 'This is me, I feel completely at home in this situation' – not so difficult, perhaps, in a simple world of small communities and living close to the land, with clearly defined roles and rituals to cope with the changes in life. Even the ravages of war and disease could be handled within a common structure like this. There was a purpose in life, however short, protected by a strong sense of order.

But the pressures of modern life fragment old certainties. It is not always easy to see where we fit in – and when we do, like Joe Lampton, it is sometimes at great cost to our personality.

People who are under severe stress sometimes wish they were somebody else, but their deepest desire is really to be themselves, to be allowed to express their own individuality without constant pressure to conform to false roles or stereotypes. Sometimes it seems that images are flashed at us from films or adverts, or stare from magazines or newspapers – a thousand images except the one that fits.

There is the recently bereaved widow who must endure endless images of happy couples; or the person battling with severe sexual problems watching yet another idealised, multi-orgasmic love scene; the fat person who flips disconsolately through catalogues of thin models, a world censored of all individuality. For such people it becomes harder and harder to feel any sense of belonging. 'It's okay to be fat so long as you're funny' – but what if you're fat and not very funny? What if you're black, have no sense of rhythm, can't sing in tune but have a brilliant debating mind which makes you a threat to white people who cling on to racial stereotypes? What if you're a white, English middle-class male but you *don't* have a stiff upper lip? What if you're a soldier but you're afraid, you're a mother but you don't feel maternal, you're deeply religious but unsure whether there's a God any more because of the terrible tragedies that have afflicted you? All around there are pressures to fit the mould shaped by social forces, by our own insecurities, by rigid stereotypes: 'This is how a man should behave, this is how a woman should behave, this is what black, white, Jewish, Irish, Muslim, Christian, Hindu people do . . .' But you don't. You don't fit. You aren't at home in the world.

Stress takes as many forms as there are individuals. And solutions cannot be prescribed like some wonder-drug to be pushed over the counter.

'Who in the world am I?' Ah, that's the great puzzle!

It's hard to solve a person. There is no pill for the pain of living, but there is learning to live with ourselves and even turning stress to our advantage. 'Knowing ourselves' is one of the keys to coping.

Of course, if we are to achieve a 'perfect fit' – or at least a closer fit between ourselves and our situation – we need to look at our environment as well as at our own personality. One piece of advice from Hans Selye to the stressed individual is to find environments which do not require 'endless readaptation'. The producer who is driven to breakdown by the endless ups and downs of her professions may need to consider whether she is *suited* to that profession. The businessman who is destroying his own health and his family's happiness by the stress of fighting a hostile take-over bid, may need to change his priorities and his job.

The stresses of the work-place, city life and financial pressures may well be important factors in our lives, but it is equally likely that the primary source of our stress lies within. It is not 'out there', but inside, in our own make up.

Type A behaviour

One of the closest connections between stress and personality was established by two researchers, Meyer Friedman and Ray Rosenmann, in the early 1960s.

They found that coronary patients behaved in similar ways – they were often very competitive, aggressive, high-achieving, impatient, restless types; people who blurted out words, firing sentences like machine guns, constantly interrupting, physically tensed-up, always trying to beat the clock. They described this type of personality as Type A. On the other hand, Type B people were much more relaxed, laid back, better listeners, not inclined to hurry or create artificial deadlines. Type B people had a much lower rate of coronary heart disease.

Friedman and Rosenmann sketched the Type A personality in their book, *Type A Behaviour and Your Heart*. When a person who scores highly on the Type A scale looks in the mirror, he may well be staring at his own worst enemy. The force that destroys his peace of mind, not to mention the happiness of many around him and may well lead to serious ill health or even early death, is a force within. His environment acts as a trigger, but he – or she – is the real problem.

Friedman and Rosenmann outline the following characteristics of a Type A personality, in their book, *Type A Behaviour and Your Heart*.

- 'Possessing the habit of explosively accentuating various key words in ordinary speech without real need and tending to utter the last few words of sentences far more rapidly than the opening words.' Friedman and Rosenmann believe the first habit reflects underlying aggression or hostility while the second 'mirrors your underlying impatience with spending even the time required for your own [Type A] speech'.

- 'Always moving, walking and eating rapidly.'
- Feeling or revealing to others an 'impatience with the rate at which most events take place'. Finding it 'difficult to restrain from hurrying the speech of others and resorting to the device of saying very quickly, over and over again, "uh huh, uh huh," or "yes yes, yes yes" to someone who is talking', urging him to hurry up. Often finishing the sentences of persons speaking.
- Often attempting to do two or more things at the same time, such as thinking about an unrelated issue when listening to someone else speak. 'Similarly, [you can be identified as Type A] if while golfing or fishing you continue to ponder business or professional problems or while using an electric razor you attempt also to eat your breakfast or drive your car or if while driving your car you attempt to dictate letters for your secretary.' Friedman and Rosenmann describe this 'polyphasic' activity as one of the most common traits of the Type A individual.
- Finding it difficult not to turn all conversation back to yourself or your own interests. At times when this manoeuvre fails, pretending to listen but really remaining preoccupied with these personal thoughts.
- Almost always feeling vaguely guilty when attempting to relax or do nothing for even just a few hours.
- No longer noticing the more interesting or lovely things encountered during the day.
- Not having 'any time to spare to become the things worth being because you are so preoccupied with getting the things worth having'.
- Attempting to 'schedule more and more in less and less time'. Making fewer allowances for anything unpredictable which

might disrupt your plans. Also having a 'chronic sense of time urgency' – a core aspect of the Type A personality.

- 'On meeting another severely afflicted Type A person, instead of feeling compassion for his affliction you find yourself compelled to "challenge" him. This is a tell-tale trait because no one arouses the aggressive, hostile feelings of one Type A subject more quickly than another Type A subject.'
- Resorting to 'certain characteristic gestures or nervous tics', such as clenching fists, or banging a hand upon a table for emphasis.

Friedman and Rosenmann also outline the following characteristics as indicating the Type B personality:

- Being 'completely free of all of the habits and exhibiting none of the traits of the Type A personality'.
- Never suffering from time urgency and impatience.
- Harbouring no 'free-floating hostility' and feeling no need to impress others with your achievements or accomplishments unless the situation demands.
- Playing in order to find relaxation and fun, not to demonstrate achievement at any cost.
- Being able to work without agitation, 'relax without guilt'.

Type A Questionnaire

The following questionnaire has been used to measure Type A behaviour. It is an adaptation of one devised by American psychologist R W Bortner.

Type A Behaviour

Circle one number for each of the statements below which best reflects the way you behave in your everyday life. For example, if you are generally on time for appointments, for the first point you would circle a number between 7 and 11. If you are usually casual about appointments you would circle one of the lower numbers between 1 and 5.

Casual about appointments	1 2 3 4 5 6 7 8 9 10 11	Never late
Not competitive	1 2 3 4 5 6 7 8 9 10 11	Very competitive
Good listener	1 2 3 4 5 6 7 8 9 10 11	Anticipates what others are going to say (nods, attempts to finish for them)
Never feels rushed (even under pressure)	1 2 3 4 5 6 7 8 9 10 11	Always rushed
Can wait patiently	1 2 3 4 5 6 7 8 9 10 11	Impatient while waiting
Takes things one at a time	1 2 3 4 5 6 7 8 9 10 11	Tries to do many things at once, thinks about what will do next
Slow deliberate talker	1 2 3 4 5 6 7 8 9 10 11	Emphatic in speech fast and forceful
Cares about satisfying him/herself no matter what others may think	1 2 3 4 5 6 7 8 9 10 11	Wants good job recognised by others
Slow doing things	1 2 3 4 5 6 7 8 9 10 11	Fast (eating, walking)
Easy-going	1 2 3 4 5 6 7 8 9 10 11	Hard driving (pushing self and others)
Expresses feelings	1 2 3 4 5 6 7 8 9 10 11	Hides feelings
Many outside interests	1 2 3 4 5 6 7 8 9 10 11	Few interests outside work/home

Unambitious	1 2 3 4 5 6 7 8 9 10 11	Ambitious
Casual	1 2 3 4 5 6 7 8 9 10 11	Eager to get things done

Scoring

Below 70	70–90	90–110	110 upwards
Type B	Type B+	Type A–	Type A

Source: Cooper's adaptation of the Bortner Type A scale

Scoring

The higher the score received on this questionnaire, the more firmly an individual can be classified as Type A. For example, 154 points is the highest score and indicates the maximum Type A coronary-prone personality. It is important to understand that there are no distinct divisions between Type A and Type B. Rather, people fall somewhere on a continuum leaning more towards one type than the other. An average score is 84. Anyone with a score above that is inclined towards Type A behaviour, and below that towards Type B behaviour.

Locus of control

Perhaps more significant than any of these factors in our vulnerability is the level of control we feel we have. We may well be tempted to say:

> 'I can't help what I feel.' 'This situation is pointless.' 'It's totally unfair.' 'There's nothing that can be done.' 'It's all very well to talk about "perspective" and "meaning" but I'm stuck with the way I am. I can't change. I'm trapped. That's the way things are.'

There is no shame in such feelings, but it is imperative to go beyond them. A feeling of total helplessness can tell us something very important about our own personality. We need to get to know ourselves a great deal better if we are to take steps to deal with the stress in our lives.

In the wake of the Type A studies, a researcher from the City University of New York, Suzanne Kobasa, developed the Hardy Personality Theory. She suggested that 'those high in hardiness will be significantly less likely to fall ill, either mentally or physically, than those who lack hardiness or display alienation, powerlessness and threat in the face of change'.

The Hardy Personality has:

- ***Commitment*** (Belief in self, in the value of what he or she is doing.)
- ***Control*** (Belief in personal responsibility and that the course of events can be influenced.)
- ***Challenge*** (A positive response to change, seeing it as a normal part of life which provides opportunities for creative decisions and growth.)

A Type A, hyper-active but hardy personality, will survive stresses better than a placid Type B who is easily disappointed by life, feeling that events are beyond his control.

There is another theory which develops this idea – 'Locus of Control'. What makes us 'tick' is not simply our basic personality, whether Type A, B, or Type B Hardy, and so on, but the fact that – in addition to our particular temperament – we have either an internal or external locus of control.

- ***Internals*** (See themselves as having some control over events. They have resources within, choices which they can make. They can respond to events and exert influence over their lives. They see themselves in the 'driving seat'.)
- ***Externals*** (See themselves as having very little influence or control. Their lives are decided by others, outside circumstances, fate, chance. They see themselves more as 'passengers'.)

The reasons for these two attitudes to life is buried in our own complex past. Whether we are an internal or an external may have something to do with how we were regarded as children by our parents. Were our ideas valued? Were we encouraged to take risks? Or were we undervalued, subject to a lot of criticism, brought up to be fearful of the unknown, scolded if we took risks? Was there consistent discipline in our household? Or was it capricious, sometimes very indulgent, sometimes too harsh?

'Externals' have often had a more insecure kind of background and are therefore less certain of their own judgement and ideas. Seeing the world as they do, as a process 'out there' beyond control, makes them more vulnerable to psychological ill health.

All this does not mean that 'internals' cannot over-react seriously to stress, if faced with a situation which is really beyond their control. The calm senior manager who organises his life into financial targets and objectives for the next twelve months, making detailed lists of appointments, dates, addresses, adding a carefully structured five-year plan, and who then loses his personal organiser, may surprise his colleagues by uncharacteristically 'falling apart'. Stress is relative to a subtle combination of our personality and our circumstances.

The following questionnaire measuring locus of control is based on the scale devised by American psychologist J B Rotter in 1966, but adapted and simplified for this book.

Locus of Control Questionnaire

Circle the number that best reflects your attitudes:

Strongly disagree	**1**
Disagree	**2**
Uncertain	**3**
Agree	**4**
Strongly agree	**5**

Our society is run by a few people with enormous power and there is not much the ordinary person can do about it.	1	2	3	4	5
One's success is determined by 'being in the right place at the right time'.	1	2	3	4	5

There will always be industrial relations disputes no matter how hard people try to prevent them or the extent to which they try to take an active role in union activities.	1	2	3	4	5
Politicians are inherently self-interested and inflexible. It is impossible to change the course of politics.	1	2	3	4	5
What happens in life is pre-destined.	1	2	3	4	5
People are inherently lazy, so there is no point in spending too much time in changing them.	1	2	3	4	5
I do not see a direct connection between the way and how hard I work and the assessments of my performance that others arrive at.	1	2	3	4	5
Leadership qualities are primarily inherited.	1	2	3	4	5
I am fairly certain that luck and chance play a crucial role in life.	1	2	3	4	5
Even though some people try to control events by taking part in political and social affairs, in reality most of us are subject to forces we can neither comprehend nor control.	1	2	3	4	5

Scoring

10–25 Internal   26–35 Internal/external   36–50 External

Source: adapted from the Rotter Locus of Control Scale

Why do some people survive stress better than others?

Despite the clear-cut Type AB analysis, researchers in more recent years have focused on the question 'Why do some people survive stress so much better than others?'

Some Type As handle the extreme stresses of their lives better than other Type As, and a Type B person may crumble under stress which some Type As would even benefit from and turn to their creative advantage.

Lifeline

Our experience of life may determine how well we cope. In a freezing winter, a vagrant who has lived for years without home or heating may survive better than an elderly person suddenly plunged into the cold because she cannot afford to pay the gas bill. When British businessman Roger Cooper emerged from years of prison in Tehran, he remarked that anyone who had survived life in a British public school, and then the army, did not have much difficulty with a Third World jail. A man who had a more comfortable (and probably saner) upbringing, might find prison in Tehran a much more difficult adjustment.

> Behind the incredible survival of the yachtsman Tony Bullimore, adrift in mountainous seas inside an upturned boat, is a life story of individualism and courage. The ability to survive against the odds does not suddenly emerge in a crisis, but has its roots in decisions and experiences from earlier life which are like miniature rehearsals for any ultimate test. Our choices, even in the ordinary and undramatic areas of life, may have more significance than we realise. The troublesome situation that we are reluctant to face in our teenage years may prove to be a 'dummy run' for something much more demanding – and the patterns laid down early will help to determine the outcome.

Perspective

Another, and more important, reason why some cope with stress better than others is that they attach a deeper meaning to their pain. They sense a purpose. Extremes of physical pain are endured by women in labour who look forward to the joy of a new baby. Their pain is 'worth it', it's a by-product not the end-product. Soldiers, too, endure levels of physical hardship and pain which might be impossible for most civilians. They have motivation, they are tough with themselves in the fight to survive and win. A soldier who loses his sense of justice or rightness in the struggle is far more vulnerable to stress. Veterans of the Vietnam War, returning to an America disrupted by peace protests, suffered from much higher levels of stress disorder than veterans of the Second World War who came home as heroes.

When our world collapses, it can take with it the structures of our beliefs. Political ideals, faith, values, come tumbling about our heads. What does life *mean* any more? What is the struggle all about? The one we loved is dead, cruelly snatched from us. The firm we served for forty years has gone to the wall. The friend we trusted has betrayed us. What is the point of going on?

This loss of direction sometimes leads people to suicide. In the former Soviet Union one Ukrainian spoke of the collapse of communism as 'people dissolving before our very eyes'. A communist official's job is wiped out overnight. His office is closed, his papers confiscated for archives. The statue of Lenin, his icon, lies smashed in the market square. In one day, he has lost livelihood, status, purpose. He faces the unknown, prosecution, even death. No wonder certain individuals have succumbed to these extreme changes by 'ending it all'.

Yet there were similar extreme disruptions of life for Soviet Jews in the pogroms and persecutions of the early twentieth century. In one day, a whole village could be destroyed and livelihoods ruined and yet, as the film *Fiddler on the Roof* dramatised, these communities often survived the worst catastrophes. The lone fiddler on the roof, still playing, symbolised the unshakeable sense of identity, of hope and shared belief. Community, rather than isolation, is a key to survival. When the significance of our lives goes beyond our individual suffering, we have a better chance of coping with stress.

Personal profiles

What is our personality? What are the influences on our behaviour? What are we *really* like? How much support do we have in times of crisis?

There are many different factors that combine to make us what we are and determine how we cope under pressure. Try writing down a personal profile. On the next page there are some questions you could ask yourself.

Temperament

- Am I the 'anxious' type or generally confident, anxious in only some situations?
- Am I trusting or suspicious?
- Do I blow up in anger or repress my feelings?
- Do I have a good sense of humour or lose it under pressure?
- On a scale of 1–10, where would I be between 'laid back' and 'uptight'?

Background

- What kind of family do I come from? Close, broken, supportive, possessive? What kind of people were/are my parents, brothers, sisters, relatives? How much am I still influenced by them? For better or for worse?
- What are the positive points of my upbringing?
- What part does class, colour, social context have to play? What values have I inherited? (Do I believe I have to move house and employ an au pair as soon as there is an addition to the family? Or do I feel isolated if I am not living near my parents? Are roots everything to me, or is it money, status? What pressures do I feel or do others put me under?)
- What moral, religious or political beliefs have shaped my upbringing? Are any of these in tension with my life now? Am I rebellious but guilty? Do I conform to my parents' ideas but feel resentful? Am I free to be myself? Am I free to fail?

Foreground

- What is the pattern of my present relationships? Am I in a dual-career partnership? How do I handle my own role? Am I sharing the burden of domestic life successfully or is it uneven and unfair? Do I feel resentful about doing too much? Am I living alone by choice or against my will? How far have I come to terms with this? How does my family situation function today and what are the main sources of stress acting upon me?
- How much support do I have in my life? From colleagues at work, family, friends, doctors, counsellors, self-help groups – do I have any support at all? Anyone to turn to in trouble or to help in a crisis? Anyone to give practical advice or to confide in or to comfort me? Do I have any strategies to help me through periods of stress, any 'support system'?

'Support systems' are so important in helping us to cope with stress that it is worth paying very close attention to this aspect of our personal situation.

Social Support Questionnaire

Think of a situation which has caused you a great deal of personal stress. To what extent did each of the following help you with the problem? 1 indicates little support and 5 a great deal of social support.

Husband/wife, partner	1	2	3	4	5
Mother	1	2	3	4	5
Father	1	2	3	4	5
Sister	1	2	3	4	5
Brother	1	2	3	4	5
Other relative	1	2	3	4	5
Close friend	1	2	3	4	5

Casual friend	1	2	3	4	5
Work colleague	1	2	3	4	5
Doctor/clergyman/counsellor	1	2	3	4	5

Scoring

1–10	11–20	21–40
Low social support	Moderate	High

Looking to the future

If you have answered all the questionnaires so far and perhaps written down a personal profile too, you may be a little clearer about yourself and your situation. But equally you may still be confused. You may still be a mystery to yourself . . .

'Who in the world am I?' Ah, that's the great puzzle!

Doctors in the ancient world believed that there were four 'humours' – four basic types – melancholic, phlegmatic, sanguine and choleric – and that all human beings acted according to type. This view persisted at least until the seventeenth century. Although we have fortunately long since abandoned such a rigid view of personality, cast into stereotypes, we still have to be careful about categorising an individual. 'Oh, he's a depressive.' 'Oh, she's an extrovert', 'He's always a good laugh' . . . Always? Always laughing, always sad, always extrovert?

No one is 'always'. And no attitude or frame of mind or habit need be for always. The only 'always' in our lives is hope.

Type A, Type B and Locus of Control are guides, often roughly drawn, which serve to point us towards the future. However handicapped we may feel by our upbringing or our temperament, we have tremendous potential for change. This is the most important thing to know about ourselves. In many ways we can break the chains of the past. We may *feel* trapped but we are not. We may think we are in a desperately dark tunnel where there is no light. But there is light. The way out begins with the first rays of that light beginning to illuminate ourselves, our history and our personality.

As we painfully but gently look at our own vulnerability – never being too hard on ourselves but always being truthful – we can make very important progress. A little light maybe, but enough to start the journey.

3 The Stress Equation

One of the most common nightmares is to be running and running, and yet going nowhere, or to see something frightening bearing down on us but to be rooted to the spot.

Nightmares are worlds where there are no choices. Life may sometimes feel like a nightmare but it isn't. We do have choices. The psychologist T Lidz puts it like this:

> 'In the transition from adolescence to early adulthood, the individual has become committed to a way of life; he has now lived it and is now mature or is unlikely ever to become mature. Now approaching the divide, he looks back and also tries to [look forward] on the basis of this experience. Perhaps he will try to climb still higher, change course while he can, or decide upon which path of descent is safest. Whether a person makes the most of the opportunity available or whether he begins to die slowly depends . . .'

It depends, not only on others, but on us.

Yet we get stuck. If stress reaches a very high level in our lives, then it may immobilise us, psychologically or physically. At the very moment when we urgently need to make a move, change our pattern of behaviour or our lifestyle, we are frozen.

The first step that an eighteen-month-old baby takes when learning to walk is the hardest. It's even harder for the victim of multiple injuries who is learning to walk *again*. Fear and pain immobilise us.

In his book *Your Erroneous Zones*, Wayne Dyer describes this state. It ranges from hesitancy to total paralysis – but it is something we can bring upon ourselves because of our deep resistance to change. It is a natural self-protection, an understandable precaution, a fear, but it stops us breaking through to solutions. He lists some typical examples of this condition:

You are immobilised when:

- You can't talk lovingly to your spouse and children though you want to.
- You can't work on a project that interests you.
- You don't make love and would like to.
- You sit in the house all day and brood.
- You don't play golf, tennis, or other enjoyable activities, because of a leftover gnawing feeling.
- You can't introduce yourself to someone who appeals to you.
- You avoid talking to someone when you realise that a simple gesture would improve your relationship.
- You can't sleep because something is bothering you.
- Your anger keeps you from thinking clearly.
- You say something abusive to someone you love.
- Your face is twitching, or you are so nervous that you don't function in the way you would prefer.

> 'All the pressure inside immobilised me from feeling free, from being a free person like I feel now. It also stopped me from enjoying my life, so that I felt I had to pretend. When you walk around with that kind of cloak of pretence, you actually are very imprisoned. You don't want people to know that you're failing, and being married to a public figure in a sense made it doubly difficult for me, because I had to exercise double pretence. So I bought myself a cloak when we came to Liverpool and for the first seven years up here I sat in the front row of the Cathedral and went to services there. Underneath that cloak, when these panics began to rise again, I would pinch myself just here on my arm. Nobody could see, of course, but I was trying to provide an alternative focus for these awful feelings and praying that it would take my mind off my terror – that I was going to go out of control. I had these marvellous fantasies that I would stand up on a

pew and turn round and face the congregation and do something stupid. I didn't know whether I'd be able to stop myself. So I hurt myself in private, which of course did nobody any good, least of all myself.'

(Grace Shepherd, wife of the Bishop of Liverpool, from the TV series, *Relax*, BBC/Prospect Pictures, 1992)

Dyer believes that it is important to cut through 'a lifetime of emotional red-tape' and above all not to blame others or circumstances for all our problems. We must take responsibility and make those first moves, however falteringly, ourselves. But sometimes the situation has become so critical, physically or psychologically, that we need medical help before there is any chance of going forward.

When we come to look at the level of stress in our lives, when we 'balance the books', we find that we are deeply in the red. We are heading for emotional or physical bankruptcy fast. We may be in that state already.

Life stress + work stress + individual vulnerability =
Stress symptoms/outcomes

Heart attacks

The outcome may be a heart attack – and there are few more effective and deadly ways of bringing ourselves to a standstill.

Mike Goldsmith describes the terrible shock of experiencing a heart attack (from the *Independent*, 17 September 1991):

'There is almost always a warning, but hospital beds and graveyards are full of people who couldn't or wouldn't recognise it. I'd had scares – what hypochondriac hasn't – but none was like the real thing.'

Mike Goldsmith had no idea what was happening to him and was extremely unwilling to admit *how* it had happened:

'Back home, after a short stay on a general ward, I tried to come to terms with what had happened to me. We have no family history of heart disease; my diet, deliberately, didn't contain much fat, and my evenings almost always included a work-out on my weight bench. The answer had to be stress. At a stress management course I'd attended a few weeks before I'd been the only one to say I had no problems. That was my problem.

I worked in local government and there had been some restructuring that had been a big disappointment for me. After the shake-up I'd had to cover two other jobs that had not been filled immediately and train new staff. [. . .] At home I had started to build a large extension to our house, involving endless negotiations with planning and building officials. Then there were the French lessons and the driving lessons I was giving my son. During the year my wife's parents had died. I had been attached to both of them.

But I had remained calm and unruffled. Everyone else might lose their cool but I was always in control. In the end my body told me where to stuff my self-control.'

Mike Goldsmith was lucky. He survived. And his impressive honesty and willingness to change his lifestyle are a striking example to follow.

Stress, if left unattended, can lead us into all kinds of physical trouble. We are then forced to focus on the illness itself rather than the root cause. All our energy is devoted to survival and recovery. We are stuck until we are well enough to adopt a new approach to life. Those of us who are in reasonable health now should not wait for such a crisis.

The stress equation looks very simple but it is not. Stress may weaken our resistance to illness, it may be a factor in making it worse, but it may not be the underlying cause. In some cases, we may be suffering from a physiological problem that is a root cause of our stress. The best known example of this is PMT (pre-menstrual tension, or PMS, pre-menstrual syndrome) – and it can come as a great relief to many women to realise that there is a *physical* explanation for the extremes of tension, irritability and even violent mood swings they suffer. Unidentified and misunderstood, this affliction can cause terrible stress to an otherwise very healthy woman and anyone in a relationship with her.

ME/CFS

One of the most mysterious and puzzling equations is the link between stress or personal vulnerability and the condition known as Chronic Fatigue Syndrome (CFS) or Myalgic Encephalomyelitis (ME). Doctors Belinda Dawes and Damien Downing discuss some case histories in their book *Why ME?*

> ‘A wife and mother, Jane was leading the typical busy lifestyle of so many people who suffer from this condition. She was involved in numerous charities and doing good works for many people. Life seemed to be going extremely well. She had a lot in her favour: a loving husband, a beautiful house, and was definitely not a neurotic housewife or a depressed middle-aged woman.
>
> Out of the blue one afternoon, the world caught fire (well, maybe not the world, but certainly the Adelaide hills), and her house was completely obliterated. Her entire life and everything she had built up were burnt away in a single afternoon. Jane never recovered from the shock and stress of this. Her health plummeted and she began to exhibit all the symptoms of classic ME.’

These symptoms include fatigue, muscle weakness, muscle pain, poor sleep patterns, temperature control disturbance, depression, lack of concentration, and muscle twitching, amongst many others. ME is a collection of symptoms, a syndrome rather than a disease. A particular stressful situation may be the catalyst for it, or a slow build-up to crisis point. An extremely stressful life can weaken resistance severely to infection. Mind and body interact negatively. Another patient of Belinda Dawes records:

> 'It became clear in retrospect that my illness had not really started suddenly, but had slowly developed over several years of increasing fatigue, anaemia, chronic ill health, coughs and colds, etc., and exhaustion from looking after two young children, a husband and a home as well as running a busy consultant job. I had been vaguely aware of being run-down, but had simply ignored it, looking down on friends who went to bed if they had a cold – I simply assumed that ill health would go away. I now realise that getting ME was probably inevitable.'

By its nature, ME tends to 'immobilise', and it can be years before the sufferer begins to take the necessary action. Often very dynamic hard-working, competitive people suffer from ME, as if the over-stretched body is forced to a last resort: 'Stop – or else!' 'Stop rushing!' 'Stop fighting!' But the stopping becomes staying – indoors, in bed, out of work. Recuperation is vital, along with the various options for medical treatment. Then, eventually, when strength returns there has to be a plan of action too:

> 'I have had to learn to say no to people asking me to do things, something I was never able to do before. I have to budget my energy carefully through the day, and had to learn to stop immediately if I show signs of having overdone it. My husband has been particularly understanding and helpful, as he himself has experienced glandular fever and its long-term after effects.
>
> Together with my husband and Dr Dawes, I reviewed my life and made changes to reduce the physical demands in my work and domestic life. I eventually changed my job, and we moved the children to a more local school.'

Some doctors have been reluctant to accept the existence of ME, and dismissive attitudes can be an additional burden to those who are suffering this overwhelming experience. Perhaps the best-known sufferer in recent years, the Duchess of Kent, has given welcome publicity to the condition, speaking openly about her own experience. A confident, extremely capable and dynamic personality can so easily conceal a situation of physical and emotional overload. The body rebels.

Physical crisis, like heart disease or a debilitating condition like ME, can creep up on us unawares. The effect of a heart attack is a sudden, shattering blow to our world which splinters beyond recognition. In the case of ME, the experience is more like a slow ebb, causing our strength to flow away as if the tide of our life were withdrawing. The effect is equally devastating on our world. We cannot live the same way again and must learn to accept our vulnerability.

There is one other example of 'immobilisation' which is one of the most fearful and generally misunderstood stress-related illnesses.

Depression

The author William Styron, in his book *Darkness Visible*, describes his own experience of clinical depression. Many would call his experience a nervous breakdown, but to Styron there are no adequate words to describe the mental anguish:

> 'Depression is a disorder of mood, so mysteriously painful and elusive in the way it becomes known to the self . . . as to verge close to being beyond description. It thus remains nearly incomprehensible to those who have not experienced it in its extreme mode, although the gloom, "the blues" which people go through occasionally and associate with the general hassle of everyday existence are of such prevalence that they do give many individuals a hint of the illness in its catastrophic form.'

According to Styron, 'depression' is a totally inadequate word for 'such a dreadful and raging disease'. He likens it to a kind of brainstorm – a term which might alert people to the extremes of fear and despair involved.

> 'Told that someone's mood disorder has evolved into a storm – a veritable howling tempest in the brain, which is indeed what a clinical depression resembles like nothing else – even the uninformed layman might display sympathy rather than the standard reaction that depression evokes, something akin to: "So what?" or "You'll pull out of it" or "We all have bad days".'

Clinical depression is not about sitting in a corner all day feeling sad. It is a truly terrifying affliction that can strike down a totally 'unlikely' victim. Although a mysterious complex of events, often involving chemical as well as psychological factors in its origin, it is vitally important to be aware that if we allow stress to go on the rampage in our lives, our minds may go on the rampage too.

Benzodiazepine addiction (see Part Two) may be a factor in some cases – William Styron now believes that sleeping tablets were a significant cause in his case – but our concern here is with the stress equation, the interlocking of circumstances and personal vulnerability, which might drive a perfectly ordinary conscientious and balanced person, one who is not chemically dependent in any way on drugs or alcohol, to find themselves right at the screaming edge.

A person suffering from a clinical depression is unlikely to be reading this book. If they are, it will be in snatches, picked up, put down, poorly remembered, blurred. It will make them angry, seem senseless, irrelevant. Their minds will flit on to something else – usually back to their condition. Which is hopeless. What book can help? They cannot, in the midst of darkness, stumble round looking for a candle. They will curse the darkness and be cursed by it.

To be in a state of depression is to be in hell. So much so that one woman, facing a terminal illness, rated her depression a worse experience. When she came through it, with the help of counselling and medication, she said, 'Now I can die without being depressed.'

> Another severely depressed woman was told the story of William Cowper, the poet, who had decided to take his own life. She listened to how Cowper had hailed a hansom cab and told the driver to head for London Bridge, where he intended to hurl himself into the Thames. But on their way, the cab was enveloped in thick fog and the driver became hopelessly lost. Eventually, he stopped the cab. 'You'll have to get out here, sir, I dare not go any further.' Cowper stepped out of the cab – and on to his own doorstep. Whether coincidence or providence, Cowper was convinced it was the latter. He sat down and wrote his famous hymn, *God moves in a mysterious way his wonders to perform*. But the depressed woman, on hearing this story, said: 'If that had been me, the fog would have cleared just before we reached London Bridge . . . God wouldn't want me to live.'

There are no glib answers to that poignant response. There are no simple solutions and no hiding from the tragic fact that depression can and does sometimes lead to suicide, the final 'immobilisation'.

Hopefully, this is not a book that offers any kind of glib answers to our minor problems, let alone a major stress-related illness like depression. The important thing here is to act early: to see the signs as soon as possible in ourselves, in others. 'Too little, too late' is so often the painful story. Whether it be a senior executive with a heart attack, a head teacher with ME or a writer suffering from clinical depression, we need to detect the signs fast. We must set up an early warning system, not a siren that blasts three minutes before the final Big Bang.

Part Two: Victims or Victors?

1 Wrong Turnings

Many people battling to survive under pressure can identify with the cry, 'Stop the world! I want to get off!' And those going through the worst personal disasters can sympathise with Woody Allen's re-write of the Twenty-third Psalm: 'Yea, though I walk through the Valley of the Shadow of Death – no, I will *run* through the Valley of the Shadow of Death'. However, sometimes our chosen escape routes lead us into far more problematic worlds than the one we are trying to leave.

Some people adopt poor coping strategies which are an attempt to escape from life, like heavy drinking, increased smoking, over-eating or literally walking away from their responsibilities. But the aim of the victor, rather than the victim, is to adopt the best possible strategy for coping: to have an effective plan of action.

Sometimes we will do anything, including killing ourselves, rather than change our old habits, like the man who read so much about the dangers of smoking that he gave up reading. However, if you have read this far . . . there is plenty of hope. There is always hope and always potential for change in every person. What is needed, first of all, is a powerful motive to change.

In the case of stress, the motive should be clear enough by now. Failure to adapt successfully, to deal with stress as it builds up in our lives, can lead to physical and mental ill-health. It frequently does, and there is every reason to deal with stress ng, long before it takes such a terrible toll.

But the motive to act, to change our lives in any way necessary, is not only negative. Another even more powerful motive is to appreciate that successfully dealing with the pressures of our lives builds our confidence. Stress is a battleground on which we can emerge victorious. We can win – even the worst stresses can sometimes be turned to our advantage. Our motive is to find a better quality of life for ourselves and for those involved with our lives too.

The first, and in many ways the most important, stage on our journey to a calmer, healthier life, is the recognition that we have a 'bias' to adopting wrong solutions. Often quite unconsciously we choose poor and even disastrous coping strategies.

In the B-movie westerns, when the hero is in trouble there is always that 'old trick which might *just* work . . .' Unhappily, our schemes for dealing with stress frequently don't work and, in fact, make our problems much worse. We need to face up to 'the old tricks', our ploys, our distractions, our habits, addictions, excuses. We need to face up to ourselves.

Anyone denying that they have a problem at all is unlikely to be reading this book. But most of us have elements of 'denial' in us. On a scale of one to ten, we might clock up three, four or even five points . . .

Denial

There are many tired old jokes about women drivers but there is nothing more tiresome for a woman than a man who will not admit that he is lost. Worse, he will not stop the car and ask for directions. As they reach the same no-entry sign for the third time running, she reasons with him sweetly, points out a newspaper vendor he could ask, but he drives off blaming the new one-way system in the town. He, of course, knows the way but the way has been 'blocked off by some morons on the council'. So now he will follow another route which he remembers very well indeed . . . and in a few minutes he will return to the same no-entry sign. He will angrily search the glove compartment for a street map which isn't there, while his wife goes to ask for directions, which is what they should have done in the first place. This classic scenario has another name. It's called denial. The man denies he is lost. His attitude of 'there's no problem' perpetuates the problem of being lost. In fact, his whole attitude is probably the reason why they got lost in the first place.

For some reason, denial is popular with men. Men are not supposed to have problems and by the time some men admit to a problem, the crisis has become blindingly obvious to relatives, colleagues, friends, the milkman, the family dog, to everyone except themselves. Denial of stress and its impact on our lives may be our way of coping in the short term, but it can have disastrous consequences – not only for ourselves but for those around us.

A husband whose wife is obsessed with a fear of cancer and fears that she has got a brain tumour every time she has a headache, will dismiss the whole problem as 'in her mind'. He may secretly scorn her weakness and neuroticism. Her fears may make him angry. The one thing he will not see is that her headaches may be genuine – but caused by stress, not cancer. In his eagerness to deny serious problems, he will deny all problems – and his wife's stress will get worse.

During the First World War, the military authorities refused to recognise the idea of battle fatigue. Many young soldiers, often no more than seventeen years old, were found wandering in a state of shock a few miles back from their regiments and the front line. These young men, who had seen the extremes of trench warfare and survived, were shot at dawn as deserters. Denial of stress-related problems can destroy lives. Ultimately, it will destroy our own. Denial is a key factor in alcoholism, eating disorders and the collapse of many relationships.

Anyone seriously wanting to tackle stress in their lives is setting out on a difficult but immensely rewarding journey. Denial is like constantly returning to the no-entry sign in the street. The person who compulsively lies to himself is a non-starter. Nobody can tell him anything. He's stuck.

There are other ways of blocking off progress, more no-entries. Here are a few:

Escapism

We all need to 'get away from it all', to have holidays, breaks, days off, escapes – but not escapism. We may enjoy escapist entertainment on television, but if we live our lives like Houdinis, escaping from the reality of our problems, we will make no progress. In the film *The Great Escape*, hundreds of men achieve a daring escape but the reality is that they are escaping into Nazi-occupied France. They are moving from a small prison to a large prison. Escapism may lead us to climb out of one box, only to find that we are in a series of 'Chinese boxes' – and we go on climbing from one to the other for the rest of our lives.

> George was always unsettled. Somehow, life was better in other places and he would regularly move job and house. His family became weary of all the upheaval. One day, he promised that they would only make one more move: to a new life in Australia. He convinced his wife and children that this was the solution to all their problems, and the whole family emigrated. But in two years, George was back in England. The long-suffering family followed, now moving into a much smaller house. Incredibly, George decided to have a second go at emigration, but not so incredibly his family stayed behind. George went off to Canada. Finally, back in England, divorced and poverty-stricken, George felt depressed. This was a shock to him because he'd always been such an optimist. It wasn't until he saw a psychiatrist that George realised that he'd been living under stress for many years and had been simply running away from himself.

> Doreen had worked for a charity. She was a tireless organiser, super-efficient, a driving personality. In fact, she drove herself to a breakdown and was forced to retire. She moved from London to the Scottish Highlands, where she soon spent her time organising numerous events in the crofting communities, herding people into activities for endless good causes, tirelessly helping others, driving herself harder and harder . . . until she had a second and worse breakdown.

The moral is, the stressed person can move house but they cannot move brain.

We can try to escape physically from our problems – and that may mean quitting jobs or marriages which have become stressful to us. Yet if we fail to look ourselves in the face, to take responsibility for the stresses within, we will be 'non-starters' on our journey. We will remain the same and, without realising it, continue to put those around us under stress.

Fantasy

As well as physical escape, we can try mental escape. It's a good way to avoid responsibility. We can fantasise about ourselves and our lives. It's surprising how many of us do.

Do you constantly dream of one particular job, or lover, or house, or spectacular win on the lottery, or piece of luck, that will change *everything* for you?

Surely there is no harm in dreaming? Or in a rush of adrenalin as we wait for our numbers to come up on a Saturday night? But, the truth is, many of us stand by wishing-wells all our lives, lost in forlorn hopes. Little or nothing changes in our circumstances, resentment and bitterness build up inside us, but we prefer to cling on to our fantasies rather than to face up to the reality of our situation.

A blurred photograph, taken through vaseline smeared on a camera lens, may make a haunting and mysterious portrait impression for an arty magazine. It will be no use in the attempt to identify a criminal. We need to identify the destructive elements in our lives clearly if we are to do anything about them.

Avoidance

We may not fantasise or dramatically try to escape from stressful situations. We may simply try to avoid them. Sometimes this works. 'I won't see that person.' 'I won't go to that party.' 'I won't write that letter.' Some people become almost pathological in their avoidance of difficult situations. They don't turn up when they are expected; they cancel at the last minute. Their friends have to make allowances for their unreliability or their well-worn excuses. Such people have more headaches and colds and suffer food poisoning more frequently than all their colleagues put together. Avoidance of this kind puts a strain on relationships and only serves to increase anxieties. As for procrastination, putting off a task which we find stressful can build up a store of guilt which becomes stressful in itself. But avoidance can also take much more subtle forms:

> Karen really wanted to do well at work but she realised that her male colleagues were threatened by her intellect. They were often sarcastic about her degree in business administration – 'Call yourself an administrator and you can't make coffee without spilling it in the saucer' – one joke after another. They liked it best when she was joking and laughing with them and playing the dumb blonde, and she was very good at that. So long as she played the part, she remained popular. But if she attracted the attention of her boss with the speed and quality of her work, then the mockery would start in earnest. So Karen chose to avoid being a success. But she became deeply resentful about playing a role that wasn't her. By avoiding success she kept the peace, but in 'keeping the peace' she lost her own peace of mind.

Diversionary tactics

Our coping strategies become 'diversions' on the journey too. We never make the real journey of discovery, because we continually divert ourselves with other worries and problems that are often only symptoms of stress. Our phobias, our illnesses, our poor relationships are 'the problem' – so we tell ourselves that if only we can avoid the fear, get the right pills, get our partner to improve his/her behaviour, all will be well.

Here are some of these unconscious 'diversionary' tactics.

Phobias

Ever since Miss Muffet was 'frightened away', spiders have had a bad name. Fear of spiders is a common complaint which at its most intense has been described as 'arachnophobia', now the title of a horror film. Assuming Miss Muffet lived in Britain, where there are no poisonous spiders, she had no reasonable cause for alarm. However, phobias are anything but reasonable – they are the complete opposite, irrational seizures of terror, which produce at their worst crescendos of uncontrollable panic.

It might seem strange to suggest that phobias – of spiders, mice, snakes, water, fire, wide open spaces, lifts (the list is endless) – are any kind of 'diversion', since they cause such distress. But they do work, in a fashion, to distract us from the real cause of our anxiety. It is often possible to avoid situations which trigger our panic, sometimes at great inconvenience (for example, climbing eight flights of stairs to avoid getting into a lift). This gives the illusion of some kind of control over the anxiety – but it is a temporary and fragile form of 'stress management'. When stress dramatically builds up in a person's life, phobias can increase in intensity and make life almost impossible to live. Extremes of agoraphobia and claustrophobia can be totally debilitating. It then becomes obvious that spiders, lifts and long, dark tunnels are not really the problem at all, but there are much more fundamental matters to deal with, which may well require professional counselling (see Part Three, Chapter 4: 'A Problem Shared').

Hypochondria

Headaches are a known symptom of stress as are stomach aches, backaches, indigestion etc. – which have been listed earlier in this book. We can add to these an infinite list of imaginary ailments. The famous rebuff, 'Not tonight, darling, I've got a headache', could be developed to 'Not tonight, darling, I've got gastro-enteritis, multiple sclerosis, a brain tumour and a rare blood disorder'.

Hypochondria is one of the things we joke about and even admit to in ourselves. What is not generally understood is that the fear of illness can be an important sign of stress. The conviction that we are suffering from Parkinson's Disease if we get a quiver in our cheek needs to be treated with gentle humour by those around us and – above all – by ourselves. However, hypochondriacs often do take all their minor ailments, aches and pains desperately seriously. They refer to their health as often as the changeable British weather, and they suffer stomach upsets, feel 'peaky', 'not quite themselves', 'a bit off-colour', 'chesty', 'fluey', and suffer 'trouble with the plumbing' as frequently as the sun goes in and out of the clouds. They are never lost for a subject to talk about, although they may eventually be lost for friends to talk to.

Underlying all this behaviour may be a deeper problem in society as a whole. It is still not so acceptable to talk about worry, stress, extremes of anxiety, as it is about other 'respectable' aches and pains. Matters are particularly confusing when genuine ailments are mixed up with imaginary ones, so a man suffering from a skin disorder and hypertension, both of them stress-related conditions, may irrationally fear he has cancer. Worry links all three. And this may be a more fundamental problem to tackle than the illnesses, real or imaginary. It is socially and personally very difficult to admit to anxiety and, in many cases, we don't even admit it to ourselves.

Projection

Projection is another of our favourite diversions. We project on to others the things we hate about ourselves. 'You're extremely selfish!' we scream. We bang our fists on the table and shout, 'How can you be so utterly self-centred? I needed the car by five o'clock!' Sometimes what we mean is, 'You haven't acted in a way that suited me.' Deep down, the truth may well be that we have organised the day precisely to fit our own needs. *We* may be the selfish ones for making unreasonable and impractical demands. But we say: '*You*'re extremely selfish', '*You* are self-centred'.

Of course, there are times – perhaps many – when our accusations are right on target. 'You're a lazy slob!' – the arrow lands quivering in our colleague's heart. He has been slacking off on that particular day, forgot to do a couple of things and is feeling guilty. Just like we are feeling guilty for getting behind schedule ourselves, but it is easier to see the fault in someone else. 'You're a lazy slob!' is easier to say than, 'I'm a lazy slob and your behaviour is a painful reminder of myself'. When we are at our most stressed it is easier to see all problems as 'out there'. We may shout at our own children for being untidy because there is a little voice in our head nagging and accusing us of untidiness ourselves, perhaps a voice that has been nagging since childhood – our mother's voice: 'Why do you always live in a pigsty!' And so it goes on, now to our own children. And if we listen carefully at their bedroom door, we may hear our children scolding their dolls and teddy bears, 'Why do you always live in a pigsty!'

Projection is like a secret vice. So secret, even we don't know it's there. We don't know it's happening, and we don't see that it's a diversion. It shifts (but only temporarily) the heavy weight of blame off ourselves. Some people are so good at projecting their anger on to others they have developed what can only be described as 'non-stick shoulders'. Whatever the problem is, it isn't theirs – it's 'Out there', 'Your fault', 'Her fault', 'The firm', 'The Government'. True, all these people and institutions may be at fault – but why do the faults bother us so much? Why does the preacher who goes on and on about sexual immorality so often turn out to be the one who has a sexual problem himself? We can learn a lot about the stresses in our lives by examining what bothers us most about other people.

Displacement

One of the most disturbing phrases of recent times is the expression 'friendly fire'. In the chaos of war, in the extreme stresses of the battlefield, allied aircraft open fire on their own side. Stress obscures our judgement and frequently blurs the target. We soon lose sight of the real source of pain and displace our anger on to innocent people or objects. We 'kick the cat' in our general fury. A wife who attempts to show sympathy to her husband after he has had a gruelling day in the office may well get caught in the 'friendly fire'.

> Tom has been bottling his anger up all day – not daring to express it to his superiors. He drives home furiously, punishing his car, hurling it round corners and swearing at other motorists. He screeches into his gravel drive. He slams the car door. He plunges his house key into the front door lock like a spear into his employer's vitals. The door bangs open, juddering against the wall. Tom's wife, Lynne, has had an extremely gruelling day herself but she says nothing when her husband comes into the kitchen and slams his briefcase on to the table, causing the china to start from its grooves on the Welsh dresser. A cup smashes. Tom swears but Lynne clears up in silence. Eventually, softly, she tries to talk to him, but Tom rebuffs her. Lynne persists lovingly. She knows that Tom had a vital meeting that day and guesses that someone higher up has blocked funding for his department. But when she asks 'What went wrong?' Tom simply snaps 'Everything!' She tries to say she feels very sorry for him but he shouts 'I don't want your bloody sympathy!' Every tack Lynne tries, Tom uses against her. Even her sympathy

annoys him. He doesn't 'project' his anger on to her, never thinking for a minute that it is her fault, but he displaces his frustration on to her. He is under stress and proceeds to put her under stress.

Virtually all of us 'displace' our feelings of aggression in various ways, on to inanimate objects as well as people. However, doors can be repaired whereas relationships sometimes can't – it takes a lot of love and patience to cope with an ongoing situation of displaced anger lasting months and years. Everyone suffers as well as the stressed person. How a family survives will depend very much on other factors, principally on the other stressors operating. If the husband and wife pictured above live in a noisy environment, have financial worries, a pregnant teenage daughter and have recently suffered a bereavement, they will fare less well than a couple who simply face a period of frustration at work. Displacement is a dangerous form of diversion. Unchecked, it will lead us well away from the aim of our journey, which is to come to understand ourselves and cope with stress creatively, not destructively.

Rationalisation

Rationalisation is a simple tactic. It means providing a good reason for what we're doing – but not the real reason.

- *I have not written that letter because it must be smartly presented and my word processor has gone on the blink.*
  (I have not written that letter because it is a tricky piece of explanation to a difficult client and I feel stressed at the thought of writing it.)
- *I smoke forty a day because my Uncle Norman smoked like a chimney and he lived to be 103.*
  (I smoke forty a day because I lost my job – before then I smoked twenty.)
- *He walks away when I'm talking to him because he hasn't got the guts to face up to what I'm saying.*

(He walks away when I'm talking to him because I'm boring and self-obsessed and he's been trying to get away for half-an-hour.)

Many years ago, *Newsweek* published a list of modern euphemisms. They included:
peacekeeper (nuclear missile);
selected out (you failed);
negative economic growth (recession);
terminal living (dying); and
negative disassembly (explosion).

On contemporary behaviour, one could add:
valuable experience (an indefinite number of mistakes);
adult movie (childish self-indulgence);
I did it my way (I'm an egotist and I'm proud of it); and
I have no regrets (I've succeeded in stifling my conscience altogether).

It's amazing how we can rationalise almost any behaviour or any situation, however absurd. We have fertile imaginations when it comes to making up excuses for ourselves; but our minds go strangely blank when it comes to thinking of the real motive for our behaviour. The truth is painful. Yet just as an accurate diagnosis is crucial for medical treatment, so honesty about ourselves is critical if we are to 'go the distance' in fighting stress.

Vicious circles

Many years ago there was a tragic potholing accident in France. Three cavers became lost in a vast system of underground caves. Eventually, their lamps failed, and all they had with them was a small box of matches. One by one they used these matches as they felt their way along the wall of a huge cavern – but they never saw the daylight again. Days later, their bodies were discovered, lying around a broad central pillar in the cave. All around the pillar was a trail of burnt matches. They had been walking round and round in circles, a mere fifty yards away from the exit shaft that would have led them back to safety.

In our emotional lives it is also possible to become trapped in a cycle of anger or despair, a roundabout of negative emotions which has exits all round – none of which we see. But it is vital for our survival that we do find a way out. Many stress counsellors, doctors and psychiatrists would agree with H G Wolff, a leading researcher into stress, who wrote: 'Of crucial importance is the need for every [person] to understand with full appreciation the truly poisonous and destructive nature of hate, resentment, jealousy, frustration, envy and fear.'

Sometimes these negative attitudes are endorsed by family and friends – and we eagerly seek accomplices on our private self-destructive journey. But these journeys go nowhere, only round and round, and the tragic victims are ourselves.

We can illustrate these 'roundabouts' by looking again at anger, which we often 'project' or 'displace' on to others. One of the major twentieth-century fictions is that 'to be able to express your anger is a healthy way to live'. This dangerous half-truth derives from the fact that depression is frequently caused by long-term repressed anger, which must be recognised – but if releasing anger (simply by itself) is so profoundly therapeutic, there should be a lot of very relaxed people in our society. Think of the people you know who 'go overboard' or have a 'short fuse', continually inclined to boil over with rage. Has there been any significant progress over the last few years? Are they feeling better, acting more calmly? Do they look healthier? On the principle that anger is good for you, there should be a lot of very peaceful and well-adjusted characters on *EastEnders* by now. But, do you ever get the feeling that over the years very angry people tend to get . . . well, just a great deal *angrier*?

When we lose our temper, we may gain a brief respite, feeling better for a while. But blowing up angrily or letting off steam at the expense of those around us is often a temporary measure for 'burning off' stress. Frequently, it creates more. Bottling up our emotions is harmful, but so is destroying everyone else's peace of mind. Our inefficient ways of handling stress have a way of rebounding on us. We can be trapped in a vicious circle of outbursts of anger, causing crises, which often lead to remorse and self-hatred, which in turn increase our irritability and produce further explosions of anger.

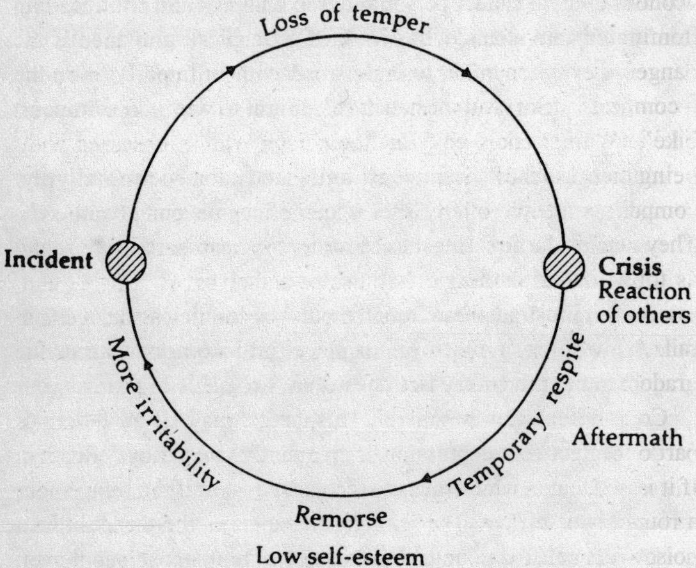

'Vicious circle' is the right phrase for this kind of horrible trap. If we do not perceive this pattern in our lives, if our 'lamps have gone out', we will simply not discover any way out. But the aim of this book is to shed light. Seeing clearly where we are now is the vital precondition to finding an exit from the circle.

Anger and aggression are perhaps the most obvious kinds of roundabout which can hinder our journey but there are other, more subtle but equally 'vicious' circles.

Competitiveness

A recent advert for sports shoes had the catchphrase *DON'T PLAY – COMPETE!* But in the game of life, play is far healthier than competition. Play means enjoyment for its own sake, competition means fighting to win. Ever since Darwin, it has been tempting to see life as that kind of struggle, and decades of free market economy, where Type A personalities in business and politics have dominated, have made the idea of enterprise and creativity dangerously synonymous with the word 'competition'. 'Don't play – compete!', 'Survival of the fittest', 'Fight to win', 'Get on your bike', 'Winner takes all'. But the person who is obsessed with being this kind of victor may well become a victim. Highly competitive people often suffer a kind of 'achievement anxiety'. They need to be first, need to be on top. A near miss is the same as total failure to them. They evaluate their lives in wins and losses. You must be on top to succeed. A second class degree is a fail. A lower profit margin is a fail. A child who does not make grade eight piano by the age of twelve is a fail.

Competition may be healthy in sport, it may be an essential part of our economy, but it is not an essential part of our identity. If it is – if that is what makes us tick – we may well be trapped on a roundabout of fear. The fear of failure is one of the deadliest poisons. It can cause untold stress, not only to ourselves but to those who have to put up with us.

Perfectionism

Many of our ways of 'coping' make things so much worse. We react to stress by creating more stress. One spiral of anguish is caused by perfectionism. Even more than competitiveness, this is seen as a good quality. 'She's such a perfectionist' is a compliment. But it can be a terrible trap. It can lead to the creation of endless false deadlines at work, too many meetings, too much paperwork. Sensible limits are not set round jobs which are relatively unimportant. The pride (and fear) of the perfectionist makes everybody continually 'run the extra mile' on their behalf.

'He's a hard taskmaster' is often softened with the words, 'It's because he's such a perfectionist'. But perfectionism may well not be the best way of achieving results. Studies have shown that Type B personalities, more inclined to go for a good rather than a perfect result, a realistic estimate of a job rather than the idealistic image of what should be achieved, are far more likely to succeed in their work. Perfectionism often leads to one job suffering terribly at the expense of another and mounting hysteria with doubtful results. Perfectionism can create a whirlpool of stress in the office.

> 'I always feel that it is dangerous to sit down and read a glossy women's magazine because what that magazine is always telling us is that as a woman you must be perfect – the perfect wife, the perfect lover, the perfect mother, the perfect daughter, aunt or sister-in-law, the perfect colleague and of course, you must be successful in your career, while remaining beautiful and a good cook all the time. Now nobody can possibly achieve that and yet that is what women are being presented with and women are very good at blaming themselves. They are excellent at blaming themselves and so, when they can't get everything right, everything perfect, they say, "I ought to have done that better", and so they are very good at creating their own stress.'

(Dorothy Rowe, psychologist, from the TV series, *Relax*, BBC/ Prospect Pictures, 1992)

As for the home, perfectionism can lead to slavery. There are the 'household gods that must be obeyed' – the vacuum cleaner, the washing-up bowl, the stair carpet and mantelpiece are extremely demanding gods. If we do not obey their commands we will fall under judgement . . . whose judgement? Our own, of course. The little voice inside us that says, 'Not quite good enough'. One woman described this as 'N-Q-W-W-W', the voice of her strict school-teacher hissing, 'Not Quite What We Want, dear!' Keeping a tidy and ordered home, leading a balanced, ordered life, are worthwhile priorities, but obsessive tidiness, hoovering, dusting, polishing, can lead to a terrible fear of invasion. Dirty cups must be whisked away from the hands of guests, cushions plumped when they get up to leave. A spot on the draining board inspires a feeling like the dreaded 'black spot' in *Treasure Island*, which means death for the victim . . . wipe that spot away at all costs or something terrible will happen. Clear the table, trim the lawn or . . . *judgement*!

> When Mary was expecting her first baby, she became frantic with worry. Worry about whether she would cope, worry about how life would change, but – above all – worry if she would live up to the ideal of motherhood. She wanted everything to be perfect for her baby. She and her husband decorated a room, hung mobiles above the expensive new cot, filled a painted chest of drawers with fluffy little jumpers and hand-knitted booties. When the baby arrived, bursting into her life with all its surprises – boy, not girl, dark not fair, blue eyes not brown, crying too much, not sweet and placid, throwing up all over the patchwork quilt meticulously sewn by Mary's best friend (another perfectionist who'd nearly had a breakdown getting it finished on time), she was in a state of shock. But Mary battled to be the perfect mother. She nearly became hysterical when the baby refused to take to the breast. She had read all the books. She knew it was best. Eventually it did, but Mary did not find breastfeeding easy and certainly not a 'delightful sensual experience'. She cursed the birth congratulation cards so neatly arranged on her mantelpiece with their silly little sentimental pictures. She hated herself for feeling anger and even hostility to the baby at times. She cried herself to sleep because she was not the perfect mother.
>
> Time passed . . . By the time Mary had her third child, she had totally forgotten about being the perfect mother. The new baby was put in the now battered cot, with a couple of ripped and off-centre mobiles. It wore a threadbare, third-hand sleep suit. Mary was far too busy looking after her other

two children to worry about the breastfeeding, which came naturally. Once, she tipped the baby out of a carry-cot on to the doorstep, but instead of frantically driving to casualty at the hospital, which she did when the first one had a tumble, she took a quick look at the baby who was still sleeping, stuffed him back into his cot and carried on up the stairs as if nothing had happened. Curiously, all Mary's friends said, as they watched the happy little boy grow up, toddling around in his patched shorts, in a chaotic house, 'He's got the perfect temperament – how do you do it?'

Obsessive-compulsive behaviour

Children enjoy inventing little rituals, like hopping over the cracks on the pavement. To step on a crack is to be 'out' or to be eaten by monsters. Children's games often have fear as well as fun mixed up together. But for complex reasons, sometimes both children and adults can develop private rituals to a disturbing and harmful degree. Perhaps the best known example is the endless hand-washing, when a man has to wash his hands hundreds of times a day. But our behaviour can become obsessional in smaller, less obvious ways too, which may not need any psychiatric help but simply breaking the circle – finding an exit. It is important to realise – and this is the hardest thing of all for a person in the grip of obsessive behaviour – that profound stresses, like anxiety, cause this. The obsession frequently becomes the only issue. If only the objects on the mantelpiece can be rearranged slightly *one* more time, all will be well with the world. If only all the window panes in the room can be counted again . . . and again . . . there will be peace of mind. However, the more the ritual is followed, the less peace there is.

This way of dealing with stress is certainly a law of diminishing returns. The more we apply the 'solution', the less we solve. The further we travel on the path, the more we go round and round in circles, like that other children's game, until 'we all fall down'. Major obsessions, like cleansing rituals, clearly need qualified help, but sometimes tracing back our behaviour with the assistance of friends and, above all, family may provide a key.

> Wendy would get furious every time her children left their coats on a bed. She did not know why, but coats on beds, hats on beds, anything flung across a bed, aroused fear and anger in her. Why did her children allow their friends to do it? Why did her husband in a moment of forgetfulness leave a shirt strewn across the duvet? Why, why couldn't people understand that this was ruining her life? Wendy would seize the offending clothes, hang them all up correctly and – in her worst fits – burst into all the bedrooms like a paratrooper looking for a terrorist. Coats, hats, gloves, a handkerchief, everything was whipped away savagely. She would even scour the bedrooms when the whole house was empty and tidy, as if fearing invasion. Wendy and her family thought she was obsessively tidy but in reality she was quite casual about the kitchen and the lounge. It was simply the beds . . . One day, after a bad week, Wendy happened to ask her mother why coats and hats had been so fiercely banned from the beds in her childhood home. Her mother's explanation came as a shock. In the deprived area where Wendy had grown up, there were regular warnings from the 'nit-nurse' that fleas were rife in the local primary school. Wendy's schoolfriends, and even Wendy herself on one or two occasions, had become infested – so, very sensibly, no clothes were ever allowed on the beds. Wendy, however, was still playing out the old ritual forty years later.

Fatalism

Among the most awkward roundabouts to get stuck on are those 'philosophies of life' which appear to be straightforward. They have the illusion of being very realistic, or even a positive way of reacting to events, but in reality they do not lead us forward at all. Tragic bereavements are dealt with by saying, 'His number came up', 'His time ran out', or freak accidents can be described as 'fate'. Even 'life' takes on a character independent of ourselves. 'Life just passed him by.' When something good or terrible happens, there's a mysterious Something or Someone up there to blame. Perhaps the most disturbing – and yet most popular – expression of this idea is the person who walks out of a plane crash as the sole survivor and announces 'Someone up there was looking after me', in spite of the fact that 'Someone up there' didn't look after the other 250 people. Such a 'fate' may smile on us one day, but frown on us the next.

This kind of 'religion' has little to do with genuine religious faith, nor does it have anything to do with a sincere humanism which sees no one 'up there' at all. It is 'fatalism' – and it is often fatal to our ability to deal effectively with stress. Earlier in the book, we have looked at the 'locus of control'. The person who has an 'internal' locus believes that 'there is always something that can be done'. He or she believes, sometimes in spite of very difficult situations, that they have considerable control over their own life and their own destiny. Things can be changed – by them. Luck can be made – by them. Circumstances can be found – by them. The fatalist, who is much more of an 'external' type, sees Life (with a capital 'L') 'out there' – ready to pass him by, ready to deal him a poor hand. 'Life' may suddenly bring good fortune but, seen from this perspective, 'Life' generally appears disappointing. People who make constant references to 'life being unfair' do not necessarily have a passionate sense of justice. They are fatalists, who believe that they have been personally 'hard done by'.

Life, of course, is not 'just' or 'unjust'. People are unjust. People can be cruel, mean and selfish, as well as generous and loving. The question is, how do we as individuals cope with the stresses of their selfish behaviour? Or with the chances and disasters in life which are genuinely beyond anyone's control? Lying behind the fatalist's outlook is often the belief that 'life owes' us something. But we owe it to ourselves to make the most of our lives. This means not blaming or crediting vague forces, but identifying problems – whether in others or in ourselves – and learning how to deal with them effectively. Above all (and this is very difficult for the fatalist), we need to take responsibility for our own lives – and accept that no one else will.

Fanaticism

The flip-side of the fatalist is the fanatic. He believes that he's got everything sorted out. He has an answer for everything. He never listens, he just talks. He is in total command of his world. He has an exaggerated sense of control over life. He has a hot-line to heaven – or a personal mission to explain his philosophy, scheme, formula, ideology. He has glazed eyes, a fixed smile, a rehearsed speech, and some very unhappy parents and friends. There are many tragic tales of people being swept up into cults, frequently when they are at their most vulnerable. Stress builds up to crisis point, with anxiety, depression, a sense of futility – a cult comes along, and suddenly the light of truth seems to dawn. Peace seems to flow like a river. Seems, but it doesn't. The river is only a mirage in an emotional desert.

Such individuals may experience temporary respite, like so many others who opt for 'poor coping strategies' – an alcoholic fog or a drug-induced trance – but beneath the mask of smiles, a young man or woman's personality is 'on hold'. They do not change, nor find deep answers. Years can be lost in a kind of time warp. This kind of brainwashing has nothing to do with true religious faith. Like fatalism, it is a substitute for that.

The deepest spirituality essentially requires growth and humility, facing up to questions as well as finding answers. It does not seek to inspire blind fanaticism or to create mindless robots. What passes for religious zeal may often be a terrible perversion of religion. The same goes for any form of political fanaticism which claims high ideals of peace and justice but has nothing to do with either.

Of all the 'roundabouts' described, fanaticism is probably the hardest to find an exit from – the hardest, but not impossible.

Sometimes a breakdown, which often happens to the victims of such manipulation, can be aptly termed a 'breakthrough'.

Dead-ends of thought

We may be anything but fanatics. We may consider ourselves 'normal' (whatever that means). We may pride ourselves on our wisdom, our balance. To put it another way, 'we've got things sussed'. But have we? Fanaticism is only an extreme way of avoiding the truth about ourselves – and that we all do expertly. The wiser we think we are, the more we may be doing it. 'A chain is only as strong as its weakest link'. A huge army can be cut off by one tiny break in its supply line. Our lives, too, can be blighted by what seems a very insignificant habit of mind.

Such patterns of thought are like cul-de-sacs – we need to reverse out of them before we can continue.

Romanticism

One of the most subtle 'dead-ends of thought' is our tendency to romanticise our lives. The most obvious form of this is the way we idealise a partner when we first fall in love, overlooking their faults, exaggerating their virtues – only to 'wake up to the truth' later on. It is better to wake up to the truth first, whether good, bad or indifferent (probably all three) and start from there. We are less likely to be disappointed by life, and much more likely to be pleasantly surprised. The woman who described her man as 'a model husband' but went on to describe a model as 'a very small replica of the real thing' has a point. No human being is ever going to be perfect and most people fall a long way short of the romantic ideal, physically, emotionally and in every possible way. The more we exaggerate and idealise, and put others on a pedestal, the more we do a serious disservice to them – and to our own ability to make good judgements and form sound relationships.

Some people's business lives follow this romantic fallacy too.

They start new partnerships with feverish excitement, they talk glowingly of their new-found friends and associates, only to be bitterly disillusioned later, 'let down', 'betrayed'. These patterns are ultimately to do with our own sense of insecurity. If we suffer from low self-esteem (which can be hidden beneath a very confident or attractive exterior), we are often on the look-out for someone who will make us feel special and become the answer to our problems. When things go well, we praise and flatter, fanning the flames of an exciting new relationship, but if things become difficult, we are very quick to blame and criticise and 'retire hurt' – again and again. There is no walk of life which is free from these hidden pitfalls, which lie beneath fragile dreams and fantasies about how life and other people 'should be'. So when romantic music starts to sweep through our minds and sunsets glow in our imagination, the next time we are assessing a new situation, we should listen hard to that familiar phrase from the movies: 'Hey – get *real*!'

Nostalgia

A close cousin of romanticism is nostalgia. Someone recently quipped, 'Even nostalgia isn't what it used to be'. We love to look back, to the 'good times', the 'good old days', especially when we are under stress now. There was a time 'before all this', perhaps in the early years of a marriage or childhood or war-time camaraderie. The old firm. The old school. The old ways. Nostalgia means literally the 'pain to return home' – but these 'homes' are in our memory and we cannot return to them except in our memory, as anyone who has experienced the disappointment of visiting a childhood home will know. Memories can inspire but they should not trap us. Living in the present is a vital factor in dealing with stress (and will be discussed in Part Three).

Regression

This is an awkward cul-de-sac to leave because regressive behaviour is a way into old methods of coping, the familiar and sometimes more comfortable devices of childhood.

> As Roger chainsmoked his way through a pack of twenty cigarettes, downed his eighth pint, and stuffed himself on chips, then had a cheesecake smothered in cream, he giggled and said to his friends, 'I'm being a naughty boy, aren't I?' 'Yes, love,' said his girlfriend, 'I'll slap your wrist if you smoke any more of those fags. Give me that pack!' 'No, shan't,' wheedled Roger, petulantly. 'You've got it coming to you tonight,' said his girlfriend. 'Ooh yes please,' sighed Roger, lighting up another cigarette. His friends collapsed laughing. A few weeks later, Roger collapsed and died of a heart attack, aged forty-two. He had been a 'naughty boy' for too long and he certainly 'had it coming to him'.

Sick humour, perhaps, but based on a true story. Which was Roger's worst problem? His chainsmoking? His excessive drinking? His poor diet? Or his way of worming out of his responsibilities by playing the little boy? Until Roger faced up to himself, he could not face up to why he punished his body so cruelly. He indulged himself and he created situations in which others indulged him.

Couples often use regressive behaviour in order to avoid conflict. It can be harmless fun and sometimes adds a touch of humour to a tense situation. But much of our regressive behaviour aims to conceal stress. We pretend it isn't there. We avoid facing up to our problems. We use regression to try to escape from ourselves.

Martyrdom

Art galleries are full of pictures of famous martyrs, some of whom seem to be enjoying themselves. The best example is St Sebastian.

He seems unfazed by the twenty arrows that have just pierced his body. He is half-smiling, standing coyly, hand on hip, and looking very blessed. Some of us suffer from the St Sebastian Syndrome. We enjoy making martyrs of ourselves. We like to manipulate others with a sense of our own sufferings. 'Don't mind me,' we say, 'I'll stay behind and clear up after you. You go out and have a good time.' 'Don't mind me . . .' What we actually mean is 'Mind me', 'Notice me', 'I hope you feel guilty about what you're doing'. But we smile cheerily. We are blessed in our martyrdom.

Yet the truth is that we are feeling hurt, but we don't want to face that stress directly. We apply indirect pressure to others, keeping up an appearance of goodwill but sighing audibly, looking conspicuously tired and wan but denying that we are exhausted. 'No, no, I'm fine, honestly – don't mind me.' Martyrdom is an old trick which simply does not work when it comes to dealing with stressful situations. It creates guilt on one side and resentment on the other. The phrase 'making a martyr of ourselves' is significant, because that is exactly what we do whilst telling ourselves that everyone else is at fault.

Repression

Repression is different from all these other cul-de-sacs because we are totally unaware of it. We may admit to behaving like a spoilt child to get our own way, playing the martyr or suppressing our true feelings. But repression is the trickiest kind of behaviour to spot. It is unconscious. We simply don't realise that we are 'repressing' feelings. They may have been hidden deep down, years and years ago. But repressing a powerful emotion like anger or fear is like trying to tread down a bulge in the carpet – however hard it is pressed down, it pops up somewhere else.

Repression can find its way out in nightmares and obsessive images, phobias, depression. To take an extreme example, some victims of child abuse simply do not remember the abuse at all. They have very poor memories of their early childhood. They have repressed emotions which are too terrible to face. But the repressed feelings can come out in many other ways and wreak their revenge on the psyche.

The notion of buried memories can be a controversial area nowadays. Some therapists have been accused of planting or encouraging ideas of abuse in their clients, and doubtless there have been such damaging cases. However, it is also beyond doubt that traumatised people do bury memories – not only in the case of car accident victims who cannot remember the accident itself, but also people who undergo shocking experiences ranging from witnessing a murder to wartime atrocities. If adults 'forget' horrors, how much more will very young children – who are even more vulnerable and have greater need for a psychological 'cut-off' – block out terrifying images? Such early, and often sad secrets, can lie behind some kinds of adult dysfunctional behaviour.

A person who is reacting extremely poorly under stress may be battling with far more than 'meets the eye'. There is no substitute for professional counselling if we suspect that this is the case.

Self-destructive behaviour

Finally, we come to the most dangerous of all reactions to stress – patterns of behaviour which, unchecked, can hurl us like lemmings over the cliff edge.

> Paula was a beautiful and talented girl. She had won an international piano competition at the age of eleven. During her teenage years she was set apart from her schoolfriends, not only because of her ability but because of her single-mindedness to succeed. But at eighteen a relationship crisis threw her into confusion. She found herself torn between conflicting loyalties – parents, piano teacher, boyfriend, all tugged away at her fragile sense of identity. She was overwhelmed by confusion and guilt. She began to hate herself for not being what everyone wanted her to be. One day, she

started to make little cuts down her arms. She began to lacerate herself whenever she felt depressed. Over a period of weeks, she scarred her arms and legs. Doctors prescribed tranquillisers, she was given counselling.

Her boyfriend, Nick, another music student aged twenty, gave her total support. Even when she landed up in hospital after a suicide attempt, he kept vigil at her bedside every night. Everyone said how well Nick was coping. Nobody could have been more loving. But sometimes Nick would come home, absolutely shattered. He would slump in front of the television, drink large whiskies and chainsmoke a pack of cigarettes. Then he would go back to the hospital at night to keep vigil again.

Everyone, even Paula's parents, agreed that Nick was 'coping marvellously' with the crisis. But Nick was attacking his own body as savagely as Paula was lacerating herself with knives and scissors. Paula's self-destructive behaviour was public and obvious. She received medical and psychiatric help. A stomach pump emptied her of sleeping pills, whilst Nick quietly continued to ply himself with an equally lethal cocktail of alcohol and nicotine. Undramatic, slow-motion suicide – Nick had adopted a way of coping that can kill. In fact, unchecked, Nick's behaviour under stress could lead to an early heart attack or cancer, whilst Paula – having grown out of her adolescent crisis of identity with the help of counsellors and friends – may live to twice his age.

Workaholism

One of the most disturbing images in Stanley Kubrick's horror film *The Shining* is the sight of Jack Nicholson, as an increasingly demented author, typing the manuscript of his novel. He has worked night and day for months to produce his masterpiece. When we finally get a sight of this work, we realise that he has been typing page after page, line after line, the same phrase: 'All work and no play makes Jack a dull boy'. Hundreds of pages are laid out with this phrase in neat paragraphs, in dialogues, in chapter headings, in brackets, in capitals: 'ALL WORK AND NO PLAY MAKES JACK A DULL BOY'. Admittedly, the author is living in a haunted house . . . but we may be haunted by our own nightmares of failure and the need to achieve.

Workaholism is an addiction and a kind of derangement – a serious imbalance in life. It is a craving, a 'need to be needed', a fear of falling short, a desire to be appreciated, an exaggerated sense of self-importance, a weakness rather than a strength of character. Work creates stress, so we must work more. Is there a problem? Work harder. Is there a crisis? Put in more hours. Research has shown that this is a dangerous false diagnosis. Ridiculous hours do not improve business efficiency. Very often, little is achieved after certain thresholds are crossed. We work an eighty-hour week at our peril. Some people – doctors for example – may be forced to work such hours, but the stress of the workaholic is self-generating. We become victims of a destructive habit which we cannot kick. We store up hidden trouble, time bombs which may explode into our emotional and physical lives suddenly and without warning. As the graffiti grimly warns: '*Death is nature's way of telling you to slow down*'.

Smoking

Cigarette packets and advertisements warn us that 'smoking can seriously damage your health . . .'

They do not tell us that 1 in 8 smokers dies of heart disease, 1 in 3 cancer deaths is smoke related, 1 in 10 smokers gets lung cancer, 1 in 5 suffers from bronchitis.

Why do we fly in the face of the evidence and *choose* to harm ourselves? Here are some of the reasons:

- We smoke to calm our nerves.
- We smoke to increase our concentration under pressure.
- We smoke to give ourselves a lift when we feel tired.
- We smoke because we feel more confident with a cigarette in our hands. It's a prop. It forms a useful barrier between

ourselves and others, a 'smokescreen'. We can tap out our ash as we make a point, retreat into quiet enjoyment of a drag as we collect our thoughts. We can conduct our own little ritual of opening packets, lighting up, waving, puffing, stubbing out. We can give ourselves an illusion of control over our environment.

- We can say 'I need a cigarette' as an acceptable sign of stress. It's okay to reach for the cigarette lighter, not okay to admit 'I'm not coping with my life today'. Cigarettes give us a feeling of coping, a temporary relief.

Smoking is a flexible habit . . . except when it comes to giving it up. The main reason we smoke is because nicotine is a drug. It is legal and it is addictive. Cigarettes are available everywhere and we're hooked.

But perhaps the hidden motive, which lies behind so much of our self-destructive behaviour, is that – deep down – we don't want to live.

> 'Of course I want to live. I love life! All right, so now and again I light up a cigarette. I enjoy it. I may smoke a few extra when I'm under pressure . . .'

But do you want to live? Severe stress sometimes weakens our resolve. Deep down, too deep to admit to ourselves, sometimes we don't care very much about our lives. Things are so bad that they can't get much worse. That was Nick's view as he watched Paula slide into a suicide attempt, and doubled his intake of nicotine and alcohol. He joined her in the downward spiral.

Alcohol

When we react to a crisis by saying 'I need a stiff drink', we start walking up another escalator that is going down. 'This will lift you', 'It'll warm the cockles of your heart' . . . Alcohol is a depressant. Ultimately, it does not lift us. It does not warm but in fact lowers body temperature. It certainly acts as a relaxant and can release us from inhibitions but it often brings to the surface feelings of anger or depression which lie hidden when we're sober. If we are sexually repressed, we may become freer, even embarrassing, when we are 'merry' – but when we are sober, we remain uptight. Drink is not a solution to our personality problems and it does not increase our ability to cope with the pressures of life. Yet drink is the 'cure-all', the socially acceptable remedy for stress. 'Get this down you', 'Go on, have another, you'll feel better'. Drink is so acceptable that phrases like 'just time for a quick half', 'I could murder a pint', 'same again please', and 'mine's a scotch' must rank along with 'terrible weather we're having' as important idioms in the English language, vital for tourists who want to know how to behave in Britain.

The logical consequences of the 'I need a stiff drink' approach can be seen in the story reported in the national newspapers in August 1991:

> A woman appeared recently in a London magistrates court charged with being more than four times over the blood alcohol limit. It was the second time in twenty-four hours the police had caught her drunk in her car. The magistrate said that the blood alcohol reading of 398 milligrammes was the 'highest he had encountered in 18 years on the bench'. Defending this former employee of a London stockbroking firm, her counsel explained that 'the event took place as a result of the break-up of a 17-year relationship with a man'.

'Ah, but' – it's easy to say – 'that extreme will never happen to me. I only drink when I socialise.' But have you noticed how much you have been 'socialising' recently? At the heart of our culture is a denial of drink problems. After all, we can laugh them off, pretend they aren't there or justify them: 'I need to relax after a hard day'. But it is hard to justify these statistics:

- Between 1950 and 1978 deaths from liver cirrhosis in England and Wales rose by 61 per cent.
- Alcohol is known to be involved in 66 per cent of attempted suicides and deaths, 50 per cent of homicides, 42 per cent of

patients admitted to hospital with serious head injuries, 30 per cent of deaths by drowning and 30 per cent of all domestic accidents.

- 17,000 people a year are known to be admitted to psychiatric hospitals because of alcohol abuse.
- One in four emergency general medical admissions can be attributed to the effects of drink.
- Over 1,000 people a year are convicted of drunkenness offences and numbers have doubled since the 1950s.
- 45 per cent of assaults and 50 per cent of murders are thought to be committed by people who have been drinking.
- Over 1,000 people a year are killed on the roads as a result of drinking and driving.
- One third of child abuse cases involve regular excessive use of alcohol.
- One third of divorce petitions cite alcohol as a contributory factor.
- 8–14 million working days a year are lost to industry due to heavy drinking.

(Figures supplied by Alcohol Concern, Wales)

Eating disorders

Another way we may attempt to produce changes in our feelings is to alter our eating habits. Slowly, almost imperceptibly, we start eating too much or too little. Compulsive eating or compulsive slimming, leading to weight problems or potentially fatal conditions like anorexia or bulimia, can be small habits at the outset.

Anorexia and bulimia are stress-related illnesses. Solutions can be found, often with the greatest difficulty and anguish over a long period of time, in slowly getting to the root of the anxiety. Eating disorders are symptomatic of other disorders.

Drug dependency

In the same way, chemical dependency upon drugs is a physical problem which usually originates in a much earlier need. The life story that lies behind the taking of drugs is often a sad history of stress handled in increasingly useless and destructive ways. Psychological dependency can be equally debilitating, even when a particular drug – like LSD or Ecstasy (a compound of amphetamines and LSD) – is alleged to be non-addictive and without serious physical side-effects. The need to stimulate feelings of happiness, well-being or heightened states of awareness by artificial means indicates a profound need and, frequently, a deep inadequacy which can never be resolved by a so-called 'mind expanding' tablet. The stresses deep within ourselves must be the focus of our concern – we need to look at our own low self-image, our vulnerability to peer-group pressure, our capacity for lying to ourselves and dismissing dangers which are well-documented.

Dealing with the problem of any kind of addiction, whether a chemical dependency or a psychological craving, becomes an overwhelming stress in itself. Short-term boosts become shorter and long-term problems become longer, as the drug addict – or the alcoholic, for that matter – descends into a world of make-believe and self-deception that makes Baron Münchhausen look like a straight-talking guy. Facing the truth about ourselves, vital if we are to deal with stress at the roots, is made virtually impossible when we are continually and pathetically avoiding being in our 'right minds'.

Tranquillisers

A word needs to be said about stress and medication.

Benzodiazepine drugs are meant to alleviate symptoms and relieve stress. There is no doubt that Valium, Librium, Ativan, Mogadon and other pills prescribed can be short-term treatments for anxiety and insomnia. But there is persuasive evidence that long-term dependency is harmful. The very drugs intended to deal with stress can cause it – and increase it – if taken for too long, in too high a dosage, and if taken as a substitute for other kinds of essential improvements in our lifestyle and situation.

Paracetamol, to take a trivial analogy, alleviates the symptoms of a stress-induced headache. It does not do away with our absurd, pressurised office or family life. Such pills do not cure our hostile environment. In the same way, benzodiazepine drugs can be taken to remove some symptoms, but the rule is that anyone relying upon such medication is unlikely to improve in the long term.

The situation is serious enough for 10,000 tranquilliser addicts in the early nineties to sue the two major drug producers in the UK – and hopefully no reader of this book will think that Valium is any kind of fundamental solution.

Although benzodiazepine prescriptions have fallen in recent decades in the UK, the record is not exactly impressive – from 30.9 million prescriptions in 1979 to 21 million in 1989. That represents a staggering quantity of pills being dished out, often by overworked GPs who simply have no other way of *coping themselves* with the pressure of demands for help.

> 'I came to use tranquillisers when I was going through a separation. I had two young children. I was becoming very anxious and very panicky. I was unable to sleep. I'd lost my appetite, I was very wound up and I was given tranquillisers to keep me calm because I was becoming very agitated. I became very addicted to them because they were helping me, in as far as I wasn't feeling any pressure. Then my dose increased and increased to the point that it was getting out of control and something had to be done about it.
>
> I would say from my own experience of the long-term use of these drugs is that there is this empty void of 20 years of their life that addicts don't know anything about. For 20 years they've felt ill. They haven't felt better. They are now having to go through the process of coming off these drugs. So the lesson is learned that the medication given to them which they thought was to help has actually disabled them, and

they're having to start their lives again without these drugs 20 years on.'

(Veronica Wall, founder of T.A.C.T., for sufferers from tranquilliser addiction, from the TV series, *Relax*, BBC/ Prospect Pictures, 1992)

No one should feel guilty or ashamed at taking these pills on a short-term basis. They may be a temporary 'lifeline' for some. But no one should get into the state of the woman, interviewed on a BBC Radio programme, who spoke of her hopeless struggle with addiction – sneaking downstairs at night and cutting one pill in half with a stanley knife. A professor of medicine warned that if nothing was done to help such people, they would go to their graves with bottles of tranquillisers beside them. A sign beside a desert road in Australia read:

Choose your rut carefully. You will be in it for the next four hundred miles.

Some of us are in a rut of 'short-term' solutions for a lifetime. And far from being healed, we are harmed by these temporary and entirely passive kinds of 'solution' to stress.

The way forward

Most of the negative 'coping strategies' we have discussed are – in a sense – passive. It is as if we float on the slipstream of events, drifting with our instincts and weaknesses and habits. 'Choices' happen to us.

Now we must learn to reverse that process. We must take charge of our lives, because how we choose to deal with stress affects us powerfully for good or ill.

Just how much our personal choices can influence our future is graphically illustrated by the research of Dr John Snarey (quoted in *Stress Relief* by Sharon Faelten and David Diamond). He conducted a survey over a number of years to see how a group of 52 young men, diagnosed as infertile, coped with this crisis in their lives. Dr Snarey divided the men into three groups, according to their reactions to the stress of this disappointment and challenge to their identity:

- The first group treated themselves as 'their own babies', directing all their energies towards themselves, often taking up body-building and other kinds of narcissistic activities.
- The second group found comfort in material substitutes like their house, garden, a car, a boat. All their energy was poured into home improvements and hobbies.
- The third group responded to the need for a child by loving other people's children. They became involved in the vicarious up-bringing of friends', neighbours', or relatives' offspring.

Tracing the groups to mid-life, Dr Snarey found that:

- 80 per cent of the group who focused on themselves in narcissism were divorced and the rest said they were unhappily married.
- 50 per cent of those who poured their energy into material substitutes were happily married, but 25 per cent were unhappily married and 25 per cent divorced.
- 90 per cent of those who cared for other children were happily married.

2 The Gift of Hope

At this mid-point in the book, in our journey through the pressures which affect ourselves and our whole society, it is worth pausing. We have looked in some detail at the wrong routes we can take. This intricate pathway through numerous 'poor coping strategies' could become like the threads of an inverted tapestry, which mean very little until we turn everything over and see, brightly and clearly, a true picture of ourselves and our situation. The fact is, there is frequently something neglected, often hidden deep down in our emotional resources, which may enable us to take a long-distance look at our own future. It is the gift of hope.

The greatest unsung virtue of our age is hope. We hear a great deal about love, courage, determination. We even hear about faith, whether in ourselves or in a religious sense, or in the potential of a society to change like South Africa. But often, before changes can happen in ourselves or others, before courage and determination and faith of any kind can be experienced, the first and most urgent need is to recover hope. The ancient Greeks had it right. When Pandora opened the box of all the world's troubles, and disasters and plagues flew through the air, there was a little figure who escaped last of all: a winged creature called Hope.

It is a mistake to regard hope as somehow an unimportant quality, and to confuse it with optimism or blind faith. Hope is the most mature and subtle of all virtues. Its opposite is not so much despair, which can afflict anyone in desperate circumstances, for even despair can become a fertile ground for discovering the tiniest seedling of hope. The true, absolute opposite of hope is cynicism. Cynicism is a hardened mental state which leaves no room at all for improvement or for anything surprising to occur. Any battle for survival, for anyone under the immense pressures of the home or the workplace, is frequently a battle against bitterness and cynicism, which are immobile, unchanging states of mind.

An associate professor of psychiatry at Harvard University, Dr Armard Nicholi, has written and lectured extensively on the issue of hope, which he calls 'the essential ingredient of physical and emotional health'. Some of the case histories he quotes in a recent paper dramatically underline the research already cited by Dr John Snarey. According to Dr Nicholi, our outlook on the world can be literally a matter of life and death:

> 'Psychiatrists have long suspected that hope fosters health, both physical and emotional. An increasing body of medical evidence documents the deleterious effect that depression and hopelessness have on physical health.
>
> A noted physiologist, Dr Harold G Wolf, writes: "Hope, like faith and a purpose in life, is medicinal. This is not merely a statement of belief but a conclusion proved by meticulously controlled scientific experiment." For years there have been clues that hopelessness often sets the groundwork for the development of organic disease. These clues have stimulated a number of scientific experiments, documenting the deleterious effects of depression and hopelessness on health. Let me mention a few from the medical literature.
>
> In a well-known experiment carried out at the University of Rochester School of Medicine, 54 patients for open heart surgery were interviewed preoperatively and several diagnosed as severely depressed. Eighty percent of the patients who died after surgery were in this depressed group! They were the patients without hope.
>
> In another study of 100 patients undergoing open heart surgery, 12 of them were diagnosed as severely depressed before surgery. *All 12* of these patients died immediately or in the early post-operative period. In both of these studies investigators found *no* relationship of the outcome with severity of cardiac disease or surgical complications. The only

difference they could find: those who died felt hopeless before surgery.

Very recently, a study at the Montreal Heart Institute reported in the *Journal of the American Medical Association* that patients hospitalized following a heart attack were five times more likely to die of that heart attack if they were depressed than heart attack patients not depressed.

So in experiment after experiment reported over the past 30 years in the medical literature, the impression, long held by doctors, that hope plays a significant role in determining morbidity and mortality, is being documented by rigorously controlled scientific experiment.

Hope fosters the will to live and the will to live fosters not only physical and emotional health but influences how we respond to medication and how well we recover from surgery, heart attacks, and other illnesses.

Yet our society generally and medicine and psychiatry specifically know little about hope. I recently took a peek in the index of my own textbook, (a reference work on psychiatry in the US), to see if I could find the word. Harvard University Press takes great pride in compiling a very complete index in the books they publish. I knew that if the word "hope" was used in the text it would be in the index. It wasn't. When I looked up the words "depression" and "hopelessness", I found some 141 pages discussing them.'

(Dr Armard M Nicholi, Associate Professor of Psychiatry, Harvard Medical School, 'Hope: The essential ingredient of physical and emotional health', paper delivered at the Bermuda Conference, 1994)

It is not the purpose of this book to define for anyone what the essence of hope, in their own situation, may be. However, Martin Luther King's words about restoring human value and dignity may illuminate our understanding of hope a little: 'What self-centred people have torn down,' he wrote, 'other-centred people may build up.' Hope is 'other-centred'. Whereas cynicism or bitterness is ultimately self-centred, hope implies something beyond our own private world. It suggests a view way past our own ego with its injuries or demands. For some people, this perspective may be caring for children and their needs; for others, it may be passionate convictions about society or change for the better; for many, hope is inextricably bound up with religious faith. Even a strictly 'scientific' view does not exclude the quality of hope. Dr Karl Meininger writes: 'In scientific circles there is a determined effort to exclude hope . . . because of a fear of corrupting objective judgement by wishful thinking. But all science is built on hope, so much so that science is for many modern people a substitute for religion.' He argues that a person cannot help hoping, even if he or she is a scientist. They can only strive to 'hope more accurately'.

However we choose to define hope, the lack of a vision beyond ourselves is clearly detrimental to our personal survival under pressure, and to the whole state of our society. An ancient writer summed it up bluntly: 'Without vision, the people perish.' One of the most eloquent books of recent times, on the issue of hope, explores the theme from a modern Jewish perspective:

> 'Many of the young people I meet – advantaged, articulate and well-educated, apparently with everything to look forward to – face the future with surprising apprehension. They are fearful about the erosion of the environment. They are anxious about their careers, knowing how unpredictably markets, technology, industries, exchange-rates and the economy can change, leaving people stranded and their life's work gone. They are uncertain about personal relationships, reluctant to commit themselves to marriage, seeing around them the human wreckage of discord and divorce.
>
> This new fearfulness was brought home to me in an unexpected way. In September 1993, Yitzhak Rabin and Yasser Arafat shook hands on the White House lawn signalling the fateful decision of Israelis and Palestinians to embark on a process of peace. Just before and after that day, I had occasion to visit a number of schools and I was taken aback by the

response of the children to the initiative. They were convinced it would not work. They were full of foreboding. Hatred and violence had scarred the relationship between Jews and Arabs for so long that they were convinced that nothing would change. The peace process was doomed to failure.

They may have been right: it is still too early to say. Certainly most of us witnessing the handshake knew the risks both sides were taking. We knew that hostility takes generations to heal, and that there would be attempts by extremists on both sides to sabotage any proposals for co-existence. The schoolchildren were not naive. To the contrary, they were formidably well informed. But they lacked one thing, without which no great initiative can be undertaken. They lacked hope. They were world-weary before their time. They had seen too many political ventures fail, too many expectations dashed. It was as if, to protect themselves against disappointment, they had grown a carapace of pessimism. They had formulated an unspoken rule: Nothing works. They had lost faith in the future.

This loss of faith has been much commented on. One politician recently called it the "new British disease: the self-destructive sickness of national cynicism". Merely calling for confidence and a willingness to trust, though, does not bring them about. There is such a thing as an ecology of hope. There are environments in which it flourishes and others in which it dies.’

(From *Faith in the Future*, Dr Jonathan Sacks, Chief Rabbi, Darton, Longman and Todd, 1995)

In his book, Dr Sacks offers his own perspective on hope, which derives above all from the quality of community and family life, along with deeply-held beliefs and values. Whatever our own outlook on the world, it is vital to consider, over the years to come, what improvements can be made to our personal ‘eco-systems’ of hope – and how our whole society can open windows on to a more hopeful world.

This book is largely concerned with our individual response to stress, and that theme is continued in Part Three: 'Finding a Way Through'. Some readers may wish to move on immediately to that section. For others, this brief respite at the 'viewpoint of hope' can serve as a preface to discussing the broader theme of Power and Responsibility.

Turn to p. 123 for the continuation of the journey through the pressures of life, 'Finding a Way Through'.

3 Power and Responsibility

Governments, employers, local authorities, all have the power to affect people's lives radically for good or ill. Anyone in authority, anyone with influence over another's working or living conditions, should be accountable in a democratic society.

What kind of world do we want? How can we build it? Sometimes the individual is up against insuperable odds. One woman, who is denied equal pay or proper childcare facilities, must bear the burden of the irresponsibility of those in authority who do not act justly. One man who is denied adequate holidays because, as a self-employed person, he cannot afford to take them, is the victim of a taxation system which allows company cars for the rich but not even one day's holiday against tax for those who are struggling to survive.

In recent years, we have heard talk of 'sick building syndrome', where employees suffer because of a poorly ventilated environment, but a society without air – justice, freedom, basic rights – is a sick society. The stress that the individual victim of injustice or poor conditions suffers is a symptom of that deeper sickness in his world.

While we have been working on the new edition of this book, there has been a profound change in the political spectrum of Britain. No one fully anticipated the extent of the landslide victory for New Labour – an election victory merely a few months old at the time of writing – nor can anyone assess the effect that this particular government will have on stress in the workplace. The non-voter who drily explained, 'I am not voting because, no matter which party I vote for, the government will always get in', is no doubt suffering from the political cynicism referred to in the previous section. But it is certainly right to hope and believe that serious change is possible.

'Believing the best', though, does not mean that we have to become in any way unrealistic. Part of the necessary realism in any personal or national strategy for improvement, is accepting that stress can be handed down from much lower levels than decisions made in parliament. The new government is committed to the Social Chapter, to setting minimum wages and maximum working hours to the benefit of workers, and to a number of issues, including paternity leave rights, which were discussed in the 1992 edition of this book. However, the will to change all sorts of areas of our lives and our work (or lack of it) must come from employers and workforce, head teachers and staff, as well as education ministers; from those working within large bureaucracies as well as from the victims of their delays and injustices. A pessimist has been defined as someone who 'has to choose between two evils and chooses both' – in this case, it might be the temptation to believe that 'governments cannot change anything', and then blaming politicians for everything that goes wrong.

Every individual, particularly anyone with a degree of influence over others, has a responsibility. This is true for older children in primary schools in their treatment of younger children, to take the humblest example. Bullying is a very serious problem (and a huge stressor in many lives) which begins in the playground and often ends up in suites of executive offices, TV companies, and even in the church. To examine some kinds of stresses in society, we need to look at the roots as well as at the branches. It is not only governments that are accountable, or 'servants rather than masters of the people'. It has to be all of us, in different ways – and the paradox of serving causes higher than our own, as part of winning our private battle against stress, is examined towards the end of this book. The pathway to deep change is not always by the most obvious route.

A brief history of stress

To understand the escalation of stress in the wider context, it is extremely sobering to review the last 30 years. Every decade this century has brought its own unique changes to our working environment. In the 1960s, Harold Wilson talked about the 'white heat of technology' transforming our lives, producing the 20-hour week. New technology was going to be responsible for a 'leisure age' allowing us to pursue our dreams, even midweek.

But instead the 1970s brought unrest and conflict, a workplace not knowing what it was going to produce or how it was going to do it. Studs Terkel's book, *Working*, summed it up:

> 'Work is by its very nature about violence – to the spirit as well as to the body. It is about ulcers as well as accidents, about shouting matches as well as fistfights, about nervous breakdowns as well as kicking the dog around. It is, above all, about daily humiliations. To survive the day is triumph enough for the walking wounded among the great many of us.'

Then came the 1980s, the 'enterprise culture', with people working longer and harder to achieve individual success and material rewards. We had privatisations, process re-engineering (American term for 'reorganisation'), mergers and acquisitions, strategic alliances, joint ventures and the like, transforming workplaces into hot-house, free-market environments. In the short term, the approach improved our economic competitiveness in international markets – but the strains started to show. 'Stress' joined 'junk bonds', 'software packages' and 'downsizing' in the modern business vocabulary – and its costs in the workplace mounted.

A few 1980s statistics suffice: mental illness was responsible for 80 million lost working days annually, at a cost to industry of about £3.7 billion; 35 million working days were lost annually through coronary heart disease and strokes, costing the average United Kingdom organisation £2.5 million; eight million working days were lost through alcohol and drink-related disease, costing about £1.3 billion.

Stress in the workplace today

So what have the 1990s brought us, and where is the workplace of the future heading? The early years of the decade were dominated by the effects of the recession and efforts to get out of it. Organisations 'downsized', 'de-layered', 'flattened', 'right-sized' or whatever euphemism anyone cares to use, to massage the hard reality of job losses. There are fewer people at work, doing more and feeling extremely job-insecure. New technology, rather than being our saviour, has added the burden of information overload as well as accelerating the pace of work, as a greater speed of response (for example, faxes, e-mail) becomes the standard business expectation. In addition, job insecurity is creating a climate of 'presenteeism', as individuals vie to demonstrate 'organisation commitment'.

'Presenteeism'

This phenomenon of 'presenteeism', an overwhelming need to put in more hours or, at the very least, appear to be working very long hours, is another dangerous symptom of the explosive degree of pressure in the workplace. The jacket on the back of the chair, the angle-poised lamp on the desk left on into the evening, the apparently (but not) harmless jibes as some people attempt to slink off to pick up the kids at 5 p.m., are all efforts to avoid 'the list' in a second or third tranche of redundancies. Many senior managers in the late 1990s are creating 'workaholic cultures'. Hours of work are equated in the minds of these executives to productivity: 'the longer the better'. Yet research has shown that for many workers these excessive hours can mean ill health at the very least, and certainly major disruption to the family. As a senior journalist recently commented, 'The workaholic syndrome flourishes here [in his newspaper]. It is assumed that everybody who wants to get on will be prepared to put the organisation first at all times. It's not good for marriages and I'm not convinced that it's really good for productivity and efficiency in the long term.'

Jeremy Paxman, in a recent article for the *Sunday Telegraph Magazine* (27 April 1997), paints a harsh picture of a society whose extreme at the top of professional life is obsessive work without morality, and at the bottom permanent worklessness without hope. He describes a generation in the City who

> 'are at their desks before breakfast and will buy or sell anything. Their achievement has been to keep the Square Mile the financial centre of Europe, to keep themselves in Porsches and second homes and swap a reputation for well-upholstered probity for a series of financial scandals. The casualties of this transformation are the millions who have no job and many who will never have a job again. In 1981, the political class greeted the news that the army of jobless had passed two million with the thought that unemployment was the consequence of high wage settlements and a fundamental restructuring of the economy. Ministers pooh-poohed predictions that the figure would rise to three million. It did . . . After 31 revisions of the unemployment figures to massage them into something more congenial, no one knows how many people are without work. Certainly, great swathes of industrial Britain have been reduced to rubble. It will be astonishing if the jobs ever return: they have gone to rolling mills in Taiwan, textile factories in Indonesia and coal-mines in South Africa. Accepting the laws of the market has meant consigning some parts of Britain to generation after generation of worklessness. If they're lucky, former steelworkers walk the dog while their wives work the till at the local cash-and-carry.'

> 'When I lost my job and knew that I hadn't got the remotest chance of getting it back, I was 55 years of age. I think the worst part, where the stresses have caught up with me, is not

losing my job – it's the after-effects of having lost it. It's going through the traumatic experiences of trying to find alternative employment and going down to your local Department of Employment office, and having to sign as an unemployed person. Now I know there are millions of people doing it now and there's been hundreds of thousands in the past, but I never saw myself having to do that. I never considered that would ever happen to me, not at the age of 55. It becomes an indignity. You seem to have lost your values. I fully understand these other people that are unemployed. I began to resent the fact that I was made to go down to the Department of Employment to sign on as an unemployed person. I was made to do that through no fault of my own.'

(Ron Henson, interviewee, from the TV series, *Relax*, BBC/Prospect Pictures, 1992)

Meanwhile, for many people in the middle of such desperate extremes – simply trying to survive in the insecure world of their employment – there are tremendous pressures to 'keep at it', regardless of the cost to emotional and physical health. These are pressures which come from above, but are also compounded by the fear that lurks within. A recent survey by Austin Knight of a million white-collar workers from 22 large UK organisations found that although three-quarters of employees sampled had contracted hours of between 35 and 37 hours a week, two-thirds regularly work more than 40 hours and a quarter more than 50 hours a week. Some 76 per cent said that continually working long hours had adversely affected their physical health and 47 per cent admitted their families suffered from their absence. Yet less than a third would 'stand up to their boss to improve family time'. (Ironically, 90 per cent of employers surveyed see long hours as a problem in terms of reduced performance and lowered morale.)

A price to pay

The 64,000 Ecu question is: 'Is working *long* necessarily working *effectively*?' The most productive economy in Europe is Germany, and all the EU reports indicate that the Germans work the least amount of hours of any of their EU counterparts. Excessive hours do not pay, in the long term. Even if this were not the case, financial rewards and productivity are scarcely the main issues (one may be forgiven for missing this simple fact during the heyday of the 'enterprise culture').

There is a price to pay for our short-sighted behaviour – and it is paid at home. Personal relationships are wrecked by our culture of long working days. The BT Forum's report, the *Cost of Communication Breakdown*, shows that by 1991 the UK had the highest divorce rate in Europe with over 171,000 divorces. Between 1961 and 1991, the proportion of people living in one-parent families increased four-fold and by 2000 the UK will have three million children and young people growing up in step-families. There are other factors involved, but the reality that nearly two out of three couples are working as two-earner couples makes long working hours an important social as well as organisational issue. It is hard to dispute the truth that the 'most precious gift you can give to your children is your *time*'. Professional people are increasingly doomed to living a lifestyle which is 'cash rich' and 'time poor'. Some of the most well-dressed people, with the nicest cars, are living below the 'time poverty line'. But this dangerous form of living spreads to all levels of income, and for many people deprivation affects every area: money, time and opportunity for change.

The freelance culture

Added to the basic pressures of our 'workaholic' environments is the sheer uncertainty that so many people face about the future. Rapid changes in the nature of work have forced a great many people into the 'freelance culture' – where 'freedom' and 'culture' are less likely to be our lot than slaving obsessively and total exhaustion at the end of the day. No freedom, no leisure, no paid holidays – and at present, no tax concessions for holidays or any statutory time-off for freelancers. Yet Britain is moving faster down this road than any other industrialised country, and new ways of protecting a more vulnerable workforce – and the nation's health – will have to be devised.

Short-term contract culture: trends

- In the last three months of 1994, 74,120 full-time jobs disappeared and 173,941 new part-time jobs were created.
- One British worker in eight is now self-employed.
- Between 1984 and 1994, the number of British women in part-time employment increased from 4.34 million to 5.25 million: the number of men from 570,000 to 998,000.
- In 1979, 43 per cent of employment in Britain was with companies of 500 people or more; in 1989, 34 per cent.
- In 1971, 41 per cent of male British workers were employed in manufacturing; in 1994, 28 per cent.

The trend towards this 'freelance or contract culture' is likely to have several obvious consequences.

1. More people will work from home, as sophisticated information technology helps create and support the 'virtual organisation'. With two out of three families dual-career, the problem of who plays what role in the family will intensify. Inevitable conflicts surrounding work and domestic space will upset an already delicate home balance.
2. More women will be employed, in all likelihood, replacing men as the main breadwinner – if employers increasingly recruit flexible workers. Women throughout their careers have worked part-time or on short-term contracts, whereas men have not. By 1994, there were five million women and 990,000 men in part-time work. Many more women than men, facing the need to balance family life with

employment, have experienced flexible working hours and can adapt more readily to this new environment.

3 Finally, those likely to survive the 'new millennium' or 'virtual organisation' will need some of the following skills: they must be able to diagnose their abilities, know where to get appropriate training in deficiency skills, be able to market themselves to organisations professionally, know how to 'network', have well-developed interpersonal skills, tolerate ambiguity and be able to manage time efficiently. Above all, they will need to sort out priorities in the context of work and family.

Stress and the law

Serious consideration of the way we live now – and how we can find a healthier relationship between our personal lives and our work environment – cannot simply depend on the enlightenment of those in authority. It may also depend on the refusal of individual employees or voters to let the 'powers that be' off the hook.

In America, this has taken the form of court cases instigated over claims for 'cumulative trauma', caused by stress at work. According to the HMSO booklet, *Mental Health and Stress in the Workplace*, 'in the state of California alone the number of mental health claims made by employees against their employers in 1987 was 29,000'. There is now a growing trend in Europe for employees to litigate against their employers for stress at work in general, and for long working hours and work overload in particular. An example of this can be seen in the Johnstone v Bloomsbury Health Authority case in the UK (as described by Earnshaw and Cooper, 1996). Chris Johnstone was a junior hospital doctor whose contract of employment required him to work a basic 48-hour week and to be available on call for up to a further 48 hours' overtime.

He alleged that, as a result of working excessively long hours, he suffered symptoms of stress and depression which were manifested through difficulty in eating and sleeping, by occasionally being physically sick from exhaustion, and by experiencing suicidal feelings. In addition to claiming damages, he sought a declaration that he could not be required to work 'for so many hours in excess of his standard working week as would foreseeably injure his health' even if this was less than the 48-hours availability stipulated in his contract. In essence, the issue was whether the 'implied term' of his contract – that his employer would take reasonable care for his health and safety – took precedence over the 'express provision' to work up to 88 hours in total. A great deal of interest in the case centred not only on what would be the final legal outcome, but also on the potential implications for the working conditions of hospital doctors and other occupational groups throughout the UK. Some 4 years later, very shortly before the trial of the main action was due to begin, the claim was settled out of court for £5,600 and payment of costs. No doubt Johnstone regarded this as a moral victory, but the lack of a ruling leaves the law in a state of uncertainty on what is clearly an important issue for cases involving longer hours.

It remains to be seen how the legal aspects of stress in the workplace will develop over the coming years. The European Council Directive on working time (93/104/EC) may become an important factor. This directive highlights a range of restrictions on night work, minimum rest periods (11 hours of rest in every 24-hour period), rest days, annual leave entitlements, as well as the better known maximum 48-hour-week provision.

Corporate initiatives on stress management

Fear of litigation coupled with spiralling employee health care costs have become powerful motivators for US companies to take action and reduce stress at work, and has led to a rapid proliferation of lifestyle and employee assistance programmes. Over 60 per cent of US worksites with more than 750 employees now offer some form of programme to manage stress. The Control Data Corporation, one of the United States' biggest corporate

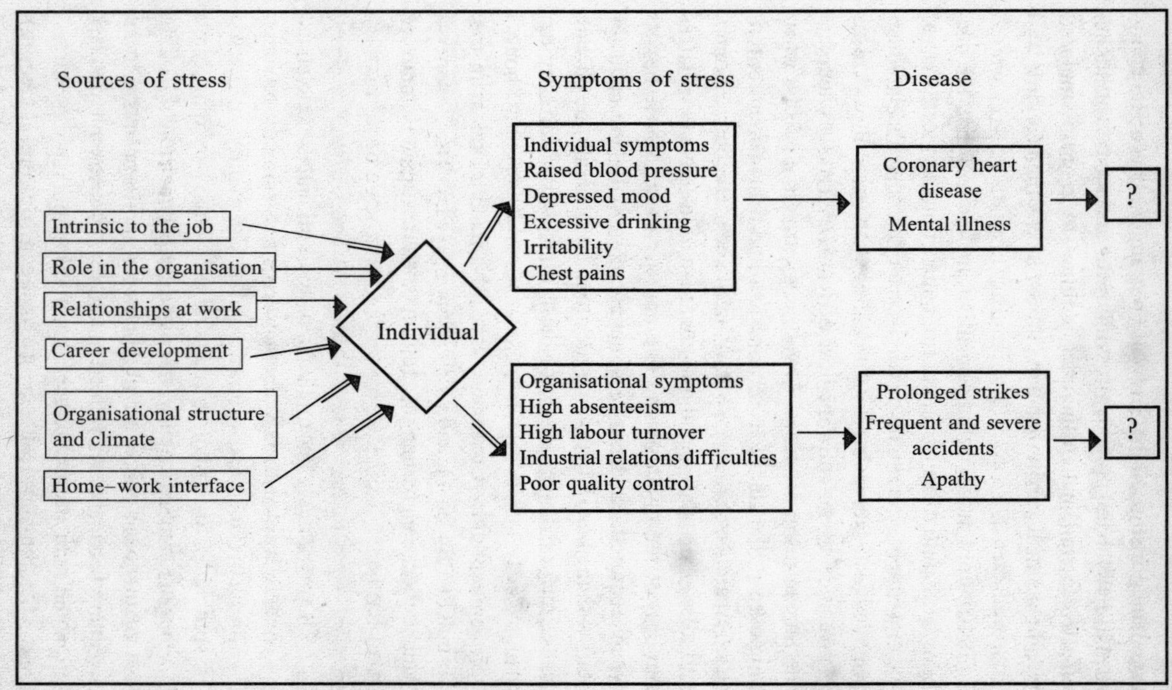
Sources of stress
Symptoms of stress
Disease
Intrinsic to the job
Role in the organisation
Relationships at work
Career development
Organisational structure and climate
Home–work interface
Individual
Individual symptoms
Raised blood pressure
Depressed mood
Excessive drinking
Irritability
Chest pains
Organisational symptoms
High absenteeism
High labour turnover
Industrial relations difficulties
Poor quality control
Coronary heart disease
Mental illness
Prolonged strikes
Frequent and severe accidents
Apathy
?
?

companies, instigated the Staywell Programme. This offers confidential health risk profiles for employees and support in taking effective action, which includes: courses to give up smoking, weight control, cardiovascular fitness, stress management and improved diet.

In Britain, a number of organisations, including the Post Office, have taken initiatives on stress and counselling services. One of the most impressive examples is at Zeneca Pharmaceuticals, which provides a six-prong strategy for dealing with stress at work. This is promoted by its chief medical officer, Dr Eric Teasdale, and the human resources team. The strategy covers all 5,000 or so employees – the chief executive officer and management; scientific researchers; production staff; sales and marketing personnel and all support staff – and aims to increase awareness of stress throughout the organisation. The approach also offers support where required, teaches stress-management skills and educates staff with the aim of improving the organisational culture, climate and efficiency. There is state-of-the-art interactive skill training, using videos, workshops, questionnaires; and counselling services are also available. Companies like BNL, Cable and Wireless, SmithKline Beecham, and many others, have launched initiatives which reflect the growing recognition that stress affects employees at all levels.

> ‘It very quickly became obvious to us all that the things that people wanted to talk about were stress-related problems: problems at home, problems related to family, to marital problems, to alcohol, to financial problems. Very quickly we began to realise that it wasn't just a simple question of looking at someone's risk of having a coronary. There were a lot of other facets that we wanted to address. People wanted to talk about their problems, people wanted help.
>
> On the physical side we've been looking at people's weights and these are coming down. People with high blood pressure are coming down quite nicely. Now we have put mental health on the agenda at all levels of this company,

from the chairman down. People are talking about it more. On any one day in the fitness centre, directors of the company and people of the shop floor are all exercising together and realising that to a large extent they are all under the same pressures. Morale has gone up tremendously.'

(Dr David Batman, group chief medical officer, Nestlé UK Ltd, from the TV series, *Relax*, BBC/Prospect Pictures, 1992)

If there is an unsympathetic view of stress-related problems at the highest levels, then symptoms of this kind of denial will make themselves known at every level. Chief executive officers may claim to thrive on stress and expect others to do so – without any of their financial rewards – but the reality may well be seen in the disordered private lives and emotionally hostile environments at home which sometimes accompany success. A redefinition of wealth, to include credits in family as well as business life and the number of loyal friends as well as offshore business accounts, might see a few hundred people fall sharply off the *Sunday Times* 'Rich List'. By the same token, a society whose inhospitable parliamentary working hours have been in direct conflict with the family life of many MPs over the years undoubtedly needs to set an example from above in making improvements. A number of women MPs, in the largest ever female intake in a British parliament, have already set this target in their sights with determination.

Human: handle with care

It is right to be compassionate towards the tragic victims of Third World injustice and good to raise millions of pounds of aid on their behalf, but perhaps Mother Teresa had a point when she opened her first Sisters of Charity home in London: she spoke for the victims of a loveless Western society, whose misfortunes were as great to her as those of the poor of Calcutta.

As individuals we need to be specific, not general, in our response to stress and make practical changes. So, too, those in authority must see clearly and act corporately, nationally. Stress is a more lethal 'virus' than many that afflict us. It pervades whole societies. It destroys lives, whether through alcoholism, heart disease, domestic violence or suicide. The pressures of environment or lifestyle can lead to the break-up of families and an inheritance of pain and insecurity for children, which in turn contributes to social tragedy. However, no amount of work-outs in the company gym or sessions with a stress counsellor can do away with the patent injustices of racial prejudice, sexual harassment or desperately difficult working conditions. Our own response to certain problems, which ultimately may have social or even legal solutions, will often be a 'holding operation'. How do I cope in the present? How can I find support in my dilemma, which has not been solved yet?

Many kinds of initiatives could be taken by those in positions of influence which could turn 'yet' into 'soon' and finally 'now'. This is where hope may be found, especially in the area of seemingly 'intractable problems' which includes pay and conditions, but goes beyond these to the fundamental questions of our whole quality of life. Such initiatives could extend to taxation policy (concessions on childcare, or basic holiday allowances for freelance workers), paternity leave, government incentives for businesses who encourage more time-protected zones for family life, and more far-reaching schemes to deal with the stress of noise pollution in public places (one train company at least, the Great Western, has launched a pioneer scheme of a mobile phone-free compartment). The fine art of dealing with stress is about careful attention to detail, in our personal and in our national lifestyle. There are major issues, like health and safety, but there are 'minor' issues too. It is often an accumulation of apparently small 'stressors' that combine to make our commuting, our working and office environments absurdly pressurised.

Any list of practical suggestions could – and should – go on for a long time. Equally important is the need to recognise the impact of stress on our society, by encouraging broad debate in the public domain, by changing the law, by instituting programmes for care in the workplace. Until stress is recognised fully as a specific and detrimental influence on health, individuals will continue to hide the truth from themselves and their employers. It may be tempting for some to regard the problem of absenteeism as did the personnel manager who posted the notice in a works office: 'All requests for leave of absence on account of bad colds, headaches, sick relatives, funerals, weddings . . . must be handed to the head of department before 10.00 a.m. on the morning of the match.' However, the harsh reality of stress in the workplace is billions of pounds lost to industry, and huge numbers of employees adopting poor and potentially fatal coping strategies, including smoking and alcohol abuse. A vicious circle of denial and destruction will continue for many unless far-sighted action is taken.

If changes do not come from the top when needed, the political and economic costs may prove (and perhaps have proved) very high to those in government. Change can be inspired by the combination of a crisis in society and the collective energy of individuals and groups who demand change. This brings us back to the theme of personal responsibility. At the turn of the millennium, we are not merely spectators at some celebration to be organised by others. We are all involved in making our own future.

Part Three: Finding a Way Through

The third section of this book offers a wide variety of practical advice for finding our way through the pressures of life, but it is worth repeating what was said in the introduction. There is no 'formula'. There is only ourselves, our will to change and some practical tips which will sometimes prove very helpful and sometimes irrelevant. Inevitably, important subjects will be treated almost in passing but these are intended to inspire further journeys of discovery.

Finding this way through will be a slow and very determined process which can begin here.

Learning to love ourselves

No amount of strategies or guidelines for survival can be a substitute for 'learning to love ourselves'. Without a strong self-image, belief in ourselves and our own worth, time management or relaxation exercises or any other advice offered here may be simply like the proverbial 'rearranging the deck-chairs on the Titanic'. The chapters that follow, in various ways, emphasise the need to build up such a belief – in some cases against the odds of past relationships which have been demoralising or destructive.

An explorer needs a survival kit, which might contain food, first aid, compass, maps and flares. Any journey through life needs at least one critical element in the 'stress survival pack': a proper and strong sense of identity.

One of the most popular ways of saying goodbye is to say,

'Look after yourself.' One way of doing just that is to give ourselves more credit, to respect our own ability to take action. It is perfectly true that we cannot cope with our neighbours, colleagues, children, relatives, spouse – or anyone – if we have a very low opinion of ourselves.

'Loving ourselves' or 'looking after ourselves' does not mean pampering the ego. It simply means finding a greater inner value, so our peace of mind does not always depend on chance, circumstances or on the moods of other people. It depends on us. Such a fundamental need cannot be provided by books. It can only be built up, perhaps with the help of books and friends and support systems. Having said that – on the way to discovering what may be a new image of ourselves – there is a great deal that can be done.

1 Taking Time and Space

Most of us, particularly Type A personalities, are afflicted with 'hurry-sickness'. The clock dominates our lives. We never have enough time. When we do have time, we do not manage it creatively. We do not take enough time before entering difficult situations, time before we speak, time before we make decisions.

'The most precious gift you can give to your children is your time' – this is enough to make any parent feel guilty, but the fact is that we don't even make time for ourselves. We need time, however little, to go gently on ourselves, to pause, to gain control. We need space too, physical and psychological, to be ourselves. We need aloneness, though not loneliness.

Most of our homes are technology traps, where the constant noise of television or interruption of the telephone add extra pressure. 'The tail wags the dog', machines become masters – our moods are controlled by the environment. The workplace is even more hazardous in this respect.

There are ways of taking time, which can also mean mental space, and using it creatively and imaginatively.

Life-planning

'Many people aim at nothing and hit their targets with remarkable precision.'

This is one achievement which this book does not encourage. On the way to gaining a much more resolute control of time and lifestyle, it may be helpful to start by considering 'life-planning'.

First of all, consider the last ten or twenty years of your life. Where were the highs and lows? The peaks of achievement or valleys of failure? Or perhaps you see the past as one even line of mediocrity, or a slide into emotional disaster? Try to visualise your life to date in the form of a graph. Draw two lines to represent your career and your personal life. A chart might look like this:

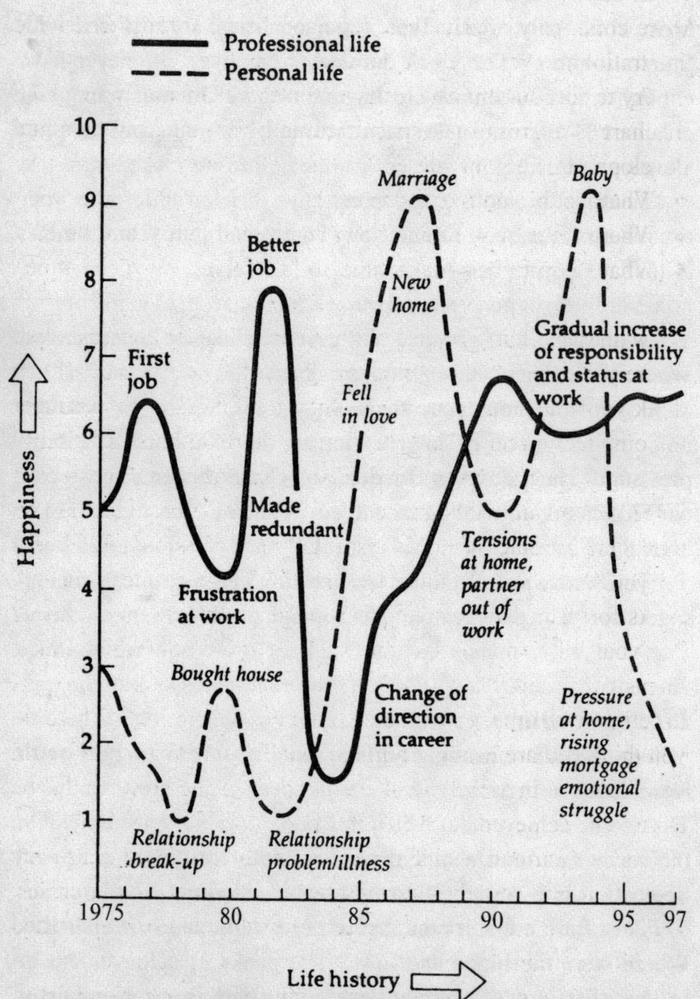

Alternatively, as suggested by Bill Pfeiffer and John Jones (in *Structural Experiences for Human Relations Training*) you could draw three curves – one for career, one for family life and one for personal fulfilment. However, it is not always easy to determine exactly what 'personal fulfilment' is – so many of us live on several levels: happy in our work, but unhappy at home; or positive about our domestic life but frustrated by lack of employment; or, more commonly, we fluctuate regularly between satisfaction and frustration in every area of our life.

Try to sort out things a little more clearly. Obviously, any kind of chart is a gross over-simplification, but look at trends and developments in your life.

- What would you like to improve?
- Where would you like to be in five years', ten years' time?
- What are your *aims* in life?

Draw another chart, looking at the future. Take an honest look at where you think your career is going over the next decade. If you think you are going to be stuck without promotion, or in danger of compulsory redundancy, or likely to increase in responsibility and status, then draw an imaginary 'prophetic' line. How would you like to change this or modify it? Can it be changed, do you think? Is this route the only way of finding professional fulfilment for you? Are there any other options?

As for your personal life, do you see trouble or stress ahead? Are your relationships showing signs of strain now which might intensify in a few years' time? Or are you perhaps looking forward to retirement, time on your own or a new start in life? Where do you think you are heading for emotionally? What situation would you like to be in at the end of another decade and how can this be assured or achieved?

These future lines, if drawn honestly on your imaginary projection, may reveal some important truths about your priorities. Perhaps there are some neglected areas of your life which need special attention urgently.

A further way of clarifying your objectives is to make a list of the ten things you would most like to achieve over the next decade – or the next few years. You could draw up separate lists for professional and personal life – but a combined list may be better. It is worth looking hard at your aims and assigning an order of priority to them.

If your aims include finding a more satisfying job, making more money, moving away from the town into the country, learning a new language, spending more time with your children and achieving greater closeness to your partner, you may find that not all of these aims will be compatible. If you want to learn a new language or improve your education, moving out of a city where there are plenty of adult education classes may not be the best idea. Making more money may well prove to be in conflict with spending more leisure time with your family.

Identify priorities and list your objectives for the future in order of their importance to you. Few of these will be achieved by luck. They need planning, discipline, sacrificing some things for the sake of others, a better-directed use of time.

Using time well is one of the principal concerns of this chapter, but it cannot be emphasised strongly enough that 'free time' – time to relax – is a key to healthy living.

Give yourself a break

Doctors are prescribing holiday brochures rather than pills to cope with the growing problem of stress, according to a report in the *Daily Express*. They say regular breaks are the only real cure to worries of the modern world, like the recession, money and work. In a survey, '83 per cent of doctors believed patients who took regular holidays had fewer stress problems'. Despite this, 'Britons typically get less holiday than most European countries – 33 days, including public holidays, compared to 41 in Germany, 36 in Italy and 34 in France.'

We can make plans for the future, plan our career, our houses, our children. But do we *plan* time off? Not simply long holidays, which need planning well in advance, but weekend breaks, days off, free afternoons, an hour to relax, to be alone. We may not be able to affect our statutory amount of holiday but we can improve its quality and effectiveness by planning. We can also learn to take spontaneous breaks – a few minutes here and there – to regain calm and control.

- ***Plan holiday breaks well in advance***. Mark them in red on calendars. Treat them like urgent appointments – with yourself. Families, particularly of dual-career couples, need VIP status.
- ***Remember well-planned short breaks*** may be more efficient for relaxation than one long and often gruelling holiday trip abroad.
- ***Avoid hyper-active holidays***. If you are a teacher, grappling with thirty-five children all term, don't turn your holiday into a school on wheels, clocking up hundreds of miles in the attempt to see yet another French château when your family would rather just 'be together' on the beach. Use holidays to counterpoint professional life.
- ***Don't turn rest days into dull days***. It has been said that some religious people take Sundays so seriously they remove the swing from the budgie's cage in case he enjoys himself. Boredom is stressful. On the other hand, don't turn rest days into drudgery days either. Some people slave away in their houses or gardens, creating more urgent tasks and deadlines. Know how to let go and if that means 'letting things go for a bit', fine. Relax. (See the next chapter on 'learning to let go'.)
- ***Take 'micro-breaks' as well as 'mini-breaks'***. Make regular presents to yourself of a few minutes. Cat-nap, if you can, or just sit back. Close your eyes. Shortly before picking up the little horrors from school or before facing a difficult situation at work, take five minutes to enjoy the calm you are about to lose. Store it up. Save the silence. A few minutes doing nothing may be more productive in our day than hours of doing something.

Learning how to turn a few moments – even a few seconds – to good use is one of the secrets of survival.

Brinkmanship

We often live life on the brink. Tempers are frayed, we can see an argument coming. How do we avert it? We are horribly late for a meeting and about to lose all sense of perspective on the day. How do we regain our composure? How do we 'pull back', 'calm down', or – as they have been saying in American sitcoms for so long – 'Chill out, man!'?

Successful brinkmanship means learning to chill out. Problems start small, moods may be triggered by the tiniest events. An actor, for example, fluffs a line on stage. The audience do not worry but he does. So he fluffs another. The audience coughs a little nervously. He senses the anxiety. It increases his. He begins to compensate by shouting too loudly or waving his arms around too much. He 'over-acts'. He ruins his performance because he has abandoned stillness and control. But the great actors, whatever goes wrong on stage, frequently establish control through stillness. They are not 'fazed'. They take time. They are in charge. The great sportsmen and women are the same. They fight back from the brink of disaster. Despite being under tremendous pressure, they 'chill out'. In a moment of calm concentration, they tap into an inner strength. They know how to win the game inside and out.

- ***Play for time***. At the moment of pressure, take your time. Take a deep breath. Pause. Think. Don't react to pressure but act upon it. Take control.
- ***Try the 'stop exercise'***. This is a very useful mental picture. When you realise that you are about to lose your calm, snap at someone, get mad in heavy traffic, over-react, behave in the way you *always* do and hate yourself for doing it – whatever the crisis – visualise a large STOP sign. See the word written large before your eyes. *STOP*. Like a car arriving at a busy junction, obey the sign. Put the brakes on. Stop. Go no further. Watch out for the dangers. Now choose your direction. Alternatively, you can imagine a set of traffic lights. It's on red. Throbbing in your mind. Stop now! Take time. Bite your tongue. Don't say what you were going to say – what you are

expected to say. Now the light is on amber. Choose your response. Change the subject, perhaps? Or refuse to rake up old scores? Or decide not to get angry in the rush-hour queue for tickets today, because it won't get you home any faster? Green light. Proceed calmly and in control.

Time management

There are many excellent books on time management. If you sense that time slips through your grasp continually then a more strategic approach, a kind of 'time-budgeting', can be a very helpful discipline. Keeping a diary for a week to see exactly how the hours of the day have been spent can give a very nasty, and healthy, shock to our system. We discover that we have no 'system' – or a very poor one. There is no doubt that a great deal of stress is caused by lack of planning which leads to endless last-minute panics. On the other hand, we mustn't make time into a god and think that we are 'wasting time' if we are not making a profit or filling our lives with so-called 'success'. The best time management books encourage planning for life – family, business, leisure. Here are two time management tips:

- ***Don't put off unpleasant tasks***. Procrastination is often a temporary 'solution' to a difficult problem. 'I'll leave it – till I've got time.' But putting things off creates more stress in our lives, on top of the problem we're avoiding. We can be burdened with guilt and the problem itself can get worse as time passes.
  - Ask yourself why you are avoiding this task. Is it fear? Laziness? You don't think it's important? You don't think it's your job? Try to identify the *real* reason for the delay.
  - Ask yourself why some things get done with such speed and enthusiasm. Why did you struggle through a busy mall of shoppers on a Saturday morning to collect a film of holiday snaps you had been looking forward to seeing and yet not spend five minutes paying a bill? Tomorrow a final demand will arrive in red. Or tomorrow a client may phone and ask why he hasn't received a letter from you. More

pressure, excuses, painful procrastination . . .
  - Then offset the unpleasant tasks with the pleasant ones. Tell yourself you will collect the holiday snaps, take a break, read your magazine as a *reward* for writing the difficult letter.
- ***Break jobs down into manageable stages***. Don't be overwhelmed by the 'mammoth task ahead'. Don't say, 'It will take months!' Say, 'The first part of this job will only take a week.' Then decide what part of the first stage you can reasonably accomplish in a day. The endless proverbs and clichés, 'Rome wasn't built in a day', 'You can't run before you can walk', 'One step at a time', 'Don't bite off more than you can chew', labour a familiar point. But the truth is profound and, like great truths, simple. Live in the present.

Living in the present

'You can't change the past but you can ruin a perfectly good present by worrying about the future.'

Learning to 'live in the present' is one of the greatest secrets of peace and one of the most ancient religious truths. But it is very hard to achieve. Animals do it naturally. A dog does not suffer from insomnia because it is worried about whether it is really up to chasing cats these days. A zebra munches grass peacefully in the wild. It does not suddenly break out in a cold sweat at the thought of being eaten by lions. Animals do not worry about the future, at least not in the speculative way that humans do. They use their memories for information and react instinctively to the present circumstances. As far as we know, a trout does not grieve over its misspent youth. But most of us humans are seriously time-warped, our bodies walking around in the present, our minds malingering in the past or anxiously contemplating a disaster which may never happen.

Beryl was in her sixties. She was a very kind and gentle woman, but there was a deep sadness in her eyes. Anyone who met her, sooner or later, would be told the tragic story of her son who had fallen asleep at the wheel of his car. His girlfriend had been killed. The boy had survived and was now living a new life, married and with children. But Beryl's mind dwelt in the past. She could not forget the grief of that girl's parents and could not stop taking responsibility for it. The memories and images of that tragedy, years ago, blighted many of her waking hours.

Beryl is trapped in a past that cannot be re-shaped. But her son, although bearing deep emotional scars from that time, is enjoying a 'perfectly good present'. Therapy and talking things over can, of course, be the solution for an obsessional worry which is rooted in the past, but in some ways Beryl is 'talking things over' too much. She is letting an endless broken record play its cracked music in her mind so loudly that she cannot hear any other tune.

It is far from easy to 'snap out' of destructive thought-patterns, but recurring cycles of images can sometimes be halted by using the 'STOP' exercise. It is worth declaring some memories a 'no-go' area, if they continually threaten to divorce us from the present. Put a barrier up, a red light, on such journeys into the past. STOP and think: 'I want to live in the present'. It may be helpful to fix on some present need or task or hope, or to turn your mind in the direction of a simple job which requires concentration, like writing a letter. Exercises to help us let go physically and mentally are discussed in the next chapter and the issue of support and counselling is raised in chapter four, 'A Problem Shared' – but whatever we do to 'clear our heads' of worries, we need to keep the object in view, which is to live in the present.

The poet Rilke had some wise advice to offer: 'Do not seek for answers . . . Try to live the questions.' Living in the present does not mean ignoring all the wounds or problems of the past but learning to live them out in the present, and asking 'How should I live today?' According to Rilke, if we 'live the questions', then one day we may 'live on into the answers' unaware of the gradual change in our perspective.

Neither obsession with the past nor anxiety about the future will solve anything in our lives. Such things will only disturb the peace of our present, which needs to be preserved so carefully. However, it is not only our thoughts which distract us from the business of living but far more often it is the relentless demands from outside.

Technology traps

The telephone

Offices and homes easily become dominated by the telephone. Telephones always have priority. A queue of people may be waiting to see us but the telephone rings suddenly, urgently. We stop everything. We grab the receiver. Crying children, hungry for their tea, must wait. Colleagues must shuffle around anxiously while we talk to an invisible person. The telephone alienates and excludes.

Of course, the telephone is a wonderful invention too, reuniting long lost friends, lovers, families, as the adverts tell us: but it is an invention. Something we have made, not our master. On the last night of the Proms, the Albert Hall resounds with people singing, 'Britons never, never shall be slaves,' but we are slaves when our lives are in thrall to a machine.

- ***You don't have to answer***. The cardinal rule, in handling the telephone, is that it does not *have* to be answered. You cannot answer if you are out of the office or down at the shops, so train yourself to let it ring whenever necessary. You have a right to be 'out' emotionally if you need peace or are engaged in an important conversation (and a conversation with a five-year-old about where babies come from is important). This does not mean ignoring the telephone or disregarding profess-ional responsibilities but – unless you are employed as a receptionist – you are entitled to give the telephone a low priority when you are facing other demands.

- ***Use an emergency code***. We are frequently worried that a call may be urgent. But how many calls are truly urgent – or genuine emergencies? Very few. Urgent callers tend to ring back quickly. You can rely on them to call again. As for emergencies, give your family and close colleagues a 'secret code' to ring you – say, four rings, then ring off, then ring again for six rings, then ring off. You answer the third time immediately. The code needs to be slightly more elaborate than the 'false start' calls that can be caused by misconnections – and might cause undue alarm. Such an emergency code may never even be used, because the odds against an extreme crisis occurring during those few times in a day or a week when you decide not to answer the telephone will be high.
- ***Invest in an answerphone***. Answerphones can be bought cheaply – at less than the cost of a week's grocery bill for many homes. An answerphone can be an investment in domestic as well as professional peace. It is a vital facility for the self-employed if they are to protect their home lives. Answerphones may well be 'horrible machines' but they are useful in dealing with another 'horrible machine' – the insatiable telephone. Remember that answerphones can be used to monitor incoming calls. You can decide if you want to answer. As for the cost of returning calls, if this is a problem, make sure your outgoing message simply asks callers to ring back at another time – 'later', 'tomorrow', 'between six and eight in the evening'.
- ***Use the telephone wisely***. If you are busy, tell the caller at the outset that you only have a couple of minutes. If you are being distracted and can't concentrate because of family pressures, explain – don't put yourself under more pressure by pretending to be calm and thoughtful when you're not. Don't be afraid to interrupt politely the 'flow' of a caller. They may have a lot of time to chat. They may need your undivided attention. Fine. Give it to them – another time.
- ***Evaluate calls***. Some calls can make a positive contribution to your day, through cheerfulness or friendship. They can give

strength. Others are routine – appointments, an electrician arranging to call – useful information to be dealt with briefly. Others bring hassle. They add pressure and they can make us very vulnerable to the stresses on the lives of others. The worries and anger of our colleagues infect our own mood. And yet the caller has no idea what circumstances we are in when they ring. Tell them, if necessary: 'I have problems here at the moment. I realise this is an important matter but I can't do the conversation justice now. Let's speak at 5.00 p.m.' Then clear space, emotionally and physically. Telephone in private, in a less stressful situation for yourself, or organise a colleague/ friend to be there to support you.

Many of our problems come from being on everybody else's agenda except our own. We need to take charge of our own lives. This is a considerable challenge, now that new technology has turned our telephones into postal services with instant delivery. Faxes and e-mails have transformed many areas of business, and our private lives, for good – but they can also increase the demands and the pace of life, as we have seen in the section on 'Power and Responsibility'. The 1960s dream of the 'white heat' of technology ushering in a new leisure age looks increasingly dated, as we rush around frantically trying to handle more communications with shorter and shorter response times. We may need to rebel against these forced agendas, above all in our own homes. We are not digital beings or a cross-breed between animals and microchips. We are *human beings*, who need to live life at a 'humane' pace and simply learn how to 'be'. That means resting, not feeling guilty at ignoring bleeps or screeds of paper churning out of a printer. It means cultivating the ability to be in – and yet out.

The telephone has been treated at length because it is an all-pervasive instrument of stress in our frantic world. Yet there is another machine, which is also rapidly diversifying in its output, bringing us a great deal of pleasure at its best, yet threatening to control us.

Television

The family has been defined as 'a band of self-seeking individuals loosely held together by the television set'.

It's a frightening scenario because it's near the truth for some people. The television is god. They are worshippers. It is a drug. They are addicts. It is all-wise. They are disciples. It is a market. They are consumers. It is an entertainer. They are the applauding audience. It is greedy for their time. They are generous in offering every spare moment they have. A caricature perhaps. But it is quite possible for a person living in the Western world to spend ten years of his or her life just watching television or videos.

Television can contribute so creatively to our lives, in stimulating us as well as providing desperately needed relaxation, that we should harness its power for our good. One of the great ironies of modern life is the number of people who switch on the television in order to 'switch off'.

This is understandable – but we also need to learn how to switch off the television in order to switch ourselves back on.

- ***We need variety in our leisure***. Relaxation need not always be taken on a drip-feed. Hobbies, sporting activities, books, music, night-classes, all engage our minds. Our psychological well-being requires us to be participators in our entertainment sometimes as well as being passive 'viewers'. Young families can be powerfully drawn together by group activities, like swimming, games, art – as well as enjoying plenty of good television. But if television is watched to excess, to the exclusion of everything else, it can isolate and impair communication in the home.
- ***Beware of using the television as 'visual wallpaper'***. Having the television on all day can be very comforting to the lonely. However, it is also a habit which may need to be checked. The stress of feeling lonely, or being plagued with worries, needs to be balanced against an invasion of sound and images into our environment which may also be stressful, although in a more subtle way.

A few years ago, writing in the *Evening Standard*, the drama critic Milton Shulman pointed out that the average American child will see around twenty-six violent incidents a day on television. Even if the viewer is not aware of watching this, the 'water dripping on a stone' effect may have a subconscious influence. Noise levels can be oppressive. Sudden changes of tempo, car chases, fights, sci-fi sound effects in cartoons – television requires this kind of pacing, often plunging us into commercial jingles at double volume, to arrest our attention which is already numbed by too many images and sounds. We can be 'wound up' by background noise – by explosions of activity in drama or by a stream of half-heard depressing news bulletins – but we can also be 'deadened' by the sheer quantity of stimuli.

Failure to react to life, feeling there is little we can do to change things, may be a hidden side-effect of overwhelming levels of information. There is a warning in the case of a soldier in the First World War who fell asleep in no-man's land surrounded by bullets whizzing by and shells exploding constantly. He had 'switched off', overcome with chronic apathy. Too much television, half-watched, half-heard, can add to a state of profound listlessness, as many long-term unemployed people have experienced. An 'overload' from a powerful medium can create an 'underload' in our own lives – a boredom that generates disinterest in the world and increases stress.

Aim for control over your life – which includes television.

The following 'rules of thumb' may be helpful:

- ***Television is a good thing*** – so don't have too much of it.
- ***Discriminate*** – decide viewing in advance. Plan watching.
- ***Love yourself*** – protect your environment from noise and tension that can be avoided by switching off or switching the volume very low.
- ***Love others*** – put relationships first. Teach children to appreciate the excitement and joys of television within sensible restraints – don't allow it to 'wash over' them or, in the long

run, become a substitute parent. The messages of television are too complex and contradictory for that task. Your input is vital to protect them from any hidden stresses there may be.

- ***Be a fan but not an addict*** – aim for so much control that you can switch off your favourite programme in the middle if a visitor, partner or child needs your undivided attention. If you pass this ultimate test . . . you can be confident that *you* are the boss.

Computer games

Controlling family screentime must not depend – as it once did – on the old-fashioned scenario of the 'piece of furniture with pictures' in the corner of the lounge. This image, which now seems a quaint memory of the fifties and early sixties concept of a visual cocktail cabinet with sliding doors, has been shattered for ever. The first step away from this simple and relatively controlled environment was the appearance of extra TVs in kitchens and adult bedrooms. Then, as prices came down, TV sets migrated to children's rooms. Then, in the seventies, came the video in the lounge; in the eighties, video stores proliferated in the high street with films to rent. Video machines 'went forth and multiplied'. One more for the children . . . or two . . . and, finally, CAME THE COMPUTER GAME. Except there is no 'finally' in this bewildering pace of development. Even to say that *Sonic the Hedgehog* has been overtaken at speed by Lara Croft of *Tombraider* is to risk being instantly outmoded. By the time you read these words, perhaps whole bedroom walls will be transformed into virtual reality zones.

Yet the same issues apply, the same technology traps – only deeper and more challenging. Playstations carry warnings about taking regular breaks to protect the eyes. But we must also protect, and encourage our children to protect, the eyes of the soul. We can recognise all the positives, the interactive skills, the imaginative richness of the best games, and do not need to become prophets of doom railing at the 'collapse of civilisation'. Computer games have given enormous pleasure to millions, and quality games have greatly enhanced the creative play of children. But any parent who ignores the dangers of over-indulgence for their children may be guilty of wanting the computer game station to be a permanent electronic nanny. It is a matter of urgent importance to limit computer game playing to a sensible proportion of time – and to also take a responsible view of the material itself. Parents with children who enjoy computer games will be well aware of the stress factors; children can often become irritable and aggressive when asked to turn off games. The physical conflicts of the game can also appear to spill over, when elder brothers hit younger brothers who disturb them, or friends who were playing happily become more quarrelsome once they've been on the computer for an hour or more. Whatever researchers may say, in this controversial area of the effect of computer games, experience is the best guide – and different children will have different tolerance levels, and quite different needs. There is no formula for sensible play; but the key issue is play, not obsession, and enjoyment, not overdosing to a point of sullen anger.

There is something disquieting about those homes which have huge lists in block capitals of 'family rules' pinned to the wall – the feeling is that the next thing pinned to the wall might be one of the children who fails to obey. However, having some general guidelines for computer game playing might be a good idea in this era of 'future shock', which so often finds us unprepared and unable to adjust sufficiently to stressful changes in our family lifestyles. Try having some unwritten rules, at least. The ideal, maybe, is to encourage children to participate in creating an agreed 'Computer Game Code of Practice'. Each family or situation will differ (some children are definitely more addictive or vulnerable than others, for example) but there may be broad principles which could be sketched out. For any single parent, or family that already feels like King Canute trying to command the electronic waves to roll back, it might be worth collaborating with other families at the local school – and suggesting some kind of school project or competition: 'Computer Game Awareness', 'the Best Guideline to Game Playing', etc. We should never underestimate the desire of children for participation in their own lives, for fair play, and for boundaries which they can respect – and which even the most badly behaved or 'difficult' children desperately need in order to feel secure. It is salutary to remember the wise words of one psychologist: 'There are no problem children. Only problem parents.' To this can be added the more quirky observation, 'Insanity is hereditary. We get it from our children.' Unless we do something to create a sensible environment for *adults* living with modern children, we'll all be barking mad before long.

Here are some notes towards 'Computer Game Etiquette for all the Family' – adjust, adapt, add, invent your own family code. The following suggestions are mainly aimed at families with children aged between 7 and 14.

First, a look at some general principles of fair play. The spirit of fair play begins with the attitude of parents. Fair play is for parents to take an active interest in the games their children choose, to play with them if possible, and to help their children discern between good, bad and indifferent material. Fair play is for parents to make sure their children visit these computer kingdoms from a position of security and loving discipline in the home, and so have no obsessive need to stay in a fantasy world. Fair play is a symptom of a healthy family life. Foul play (addictive or aggressive behaviour) is more than a potential side effect of computer games. It is a symptom of a wider problem in family life which needs to be addressed first. Fair play means parents and children both taking their share of responsibility for the quality of family life.

Now an attempt at a rough 'charter' for all the family:

- The computer game station is a servant not a master.
- It is not a force which must be obeyed – it is a game to be *played*.
- Like all games, there are rules of fair play and foul.
- *Fair play* is for children to balance game playing with many other activities – and to accept that the computer game is only one of these activities.

- Fair play is for parents to set time limits without being inflexible or harsh; to look at each situation in turn and to recognise that, when friends come and two or three players are involved, more time may be needed.
- Fair play is for parents to give advance warning that the game must finish soon. 'This is your fifteen minute call', 'This is your five minute call', etc.
- Fair play is for parents to give children the dignity of switching on and off their own games within the agreed time limits.
- *Foul play* is to become aggressive or rude to parents who set reasonable limits on time.
- Foul play is to argue that a level must be completed when it can be left on hold during a meal break, or a game must be finished when in reality this will take days.
- Foul play is for parents to burst into a room and switch the machine off in the middle of a game, without any previous warning.
- Foul play is for children to go on playing after the final 'whistle has blown'.
- Foul play is to let aggression spill from the game into the home. Repeated quarrelling, abusive behaviour or fighting is a red card. Instant switch off. Period of suspension.
- Fair play is for parents to exercise their own discretion over new material coming into the home, and to reserve an ultimate right of veto over games they consider to be harmful.
- Fair play is to work through partnership, discussion and trust, creating a climate where vetos are an unlikely last resort, and where playing bans are exceptional.

Such guidelines can be developed, at least verbally, for many different situations or to suit different family dynamics. There are so many developments in technology that creative thinking is almost a constant process. 'Surfing the net' is even more complex because there is so much (among the trivia) of enormous value, and so many educational possibilities. The snag is time – and time values. 'All work and no play makes Jack a dull boy', and

'All Internet and no exercise makes Jack a clever nerd with poor social skills and a weight problem.'

The saturation bombing of the senses

But 'information overload' is not simply a problem of cyberspace or our private mental worlds; it is now a way of life which affects even the most apparently innocuous environments. Old pubs were once places of armchairs, log fires, and slow drinking. New pubs are often restless oceans of noise, a multi-screen TV nobody is watching, bagatelle machines, one-armed bandits, pool tables, meaningless half-heard jingles and news bulletins on Radio 1, music, chat – incessant noise. People drinking hard and fast. We cannot control such environments, but when our own homes become sensory war zones, there really is no refuge. When there is no quality time with our children or enough opportunity to give them our quiet, undivided attention, they can gradually become orphans of the environment, to be adopted by whoever or whatever is bombarding them most relentlessly. Rob Parsons, in the book, *The Sixty Minute Father*, makes the point vividly that time and planning are needed to pass on the most important values to children – in the face of intense competition.

> 'In the film *True Lies* Arnold Schwarzenegger has a teenage daughter that he is finding hard to control. One of his colleagues from work explains why he may be finding it so difficult. "You're not her parents any more. Her parents are Axl Rose [the lead singer of 'Guns'n'Roses'] and Madonna. Don't think that the five minutes you spend with her can compete with that kind of bombardment."
>
> If we want our children to accept our values, we have to pass them on . . . If I have things that I believe are right and wrong I have to let them know what these are. They may reject those values, but if they matter to me, I dare not leave it just to others to teach them. Of course, much of this teaching happens informally, day by day, as they see how we

> react to situations. In fact the frightening thing is that with children values are more caught than taught. But there will always need to be conversations, debates, and guidance, and all of that takes planning and time.'

If all the time is spent on the computer or in front of the TV set, we should not be surprised if ultimately we feel like aliens in our children's world. They have been aliens in ours for far too long.

Instead of falling into our technology traps, creating stress, we need to use our inventions for good wherever possible. The future will bring more possibilities and more potential for stress too. 'Video telephones' are coming on to the market and, along with the delight of seeing our loved ones, troublesome callers will soon be able to gatecrash our lives in vision as well as sound. Despite the provision of 'self-view' buttons, allowing us to check our appearance before making calls, we may well feel more exposed and more pressurised to keep up appearances even when we are at home.

Most of our technical advances have 'pluses' and 'minuses' which we need to discern, and discover what can be turned to advantage. Wristwatch alarms can be set to remind us of an appointment or allow us to sleep on a fifty-minute train journey. But why let them go off on the hour, every hour, including when we are at the theatre or, more disturbingly, even when making love? Having a good time frequently means forgetting about time altogether.

Protection zones

Mealtimes

A great deal is said these days about what we should eat – but not so much about the *way* we should eat. Yet in our 'breakfast bar world', when we eat hurriedly and often in isolation from each other, we miss the celebration which is part of so many other cultures. We don't have *time* to be together. We are too busy to share our meals. We 'snatch' breakfast, stand around with toast in one hand, telephone in the other, television blaring, children quarrelling. We stuff sandwiches into our mouths in isolation at lunchtime, reading a paper and not noticing what we are eating, or bolt down our meals in a noisy canteen. We slump into our armchairs at night with trays of food on our laps, watching the news and spilling spaghetti down our clothes. Perhaps this depressing scenario doesn't apply to you – these meals which aren't meals so much as 'food intake', when we are always doing something other than eating, being together and sharing a common life – but Type A personalities are notoriously bad at simply 'being'. They'd rather live life on the run, preferring 'polyphasic activity', doing everything at once, to stillness. If they stuck a hot dog in their ear, ate the car telephone and poured hot coffee into the cassette machine, they'd be too busy to notice . . .

Eating should not add to our stresses but bring calm, refreshment, space, a sense of free time and quiet control into our lives. There are no rules, only our own preferences. But perhaps the ideal is at least one meal a day declared as a 'protected zone' – free from telephones, computer games, interruption and rush. Thirty minutes of quality time is better than sixty minutes of chaos and indigestion.

Privacy

It is extremely difficult to find privacy in many homes or flats, but even a corner of a room – perhaps a bedroom – with a little table and a lamp can become a 'bolt-hole'. We need somewhere to go for a few minutes when the pressures are too much. Even an unused area of an upstairs landing, screened off, can provide a capsule – if not of quiet, certainly of privacy. A space like this can provide a precious retreat, perhaps in a rare moment when children are playing quietly or a few minutes of respite from a busy schedule in the evening. We can steal some calm, even if it is in the eye of the storm. An area like this can be the physical equivalent of the 'STOP' exercise. A place of recollection, where we spend a few minutes, just a few moments of privacy. Even when we live alone and perhaps long for company and distraction, a little 'island retreat' within our environment can be a way of briefly stepping aside from our worries. We may form the valuable habit of quietening our minds whenever we are in this particular chair, by this window or in this reserved space, perhaps enjoying the silence, reading a poem, a few pages of a novel, relaxing with a magazine or a book of cartoons, listening through headphones to a song or just gazing through a window on to a street – these restful moments mean we can be our own selves, so we can come alive for a few minutes, separate from all our external demands.

Lighting

One way of creating areas, even in a confined space, is by the judicious use of light. It is true that sufferers from SAD (Seasonal Affective Disorder) need to improve dramatically the quantity and quality of light in their lives, but many of us suffer in lesser ways from a surplus of glaring white light. Hard, artificial light can add to the stress of our environment. At least at home we can exercise greater control. Most people would prefer a candlelit rather than a fluorescent-lit dinner. Why wait for birthdays and anniversaries and meals in restaurants to enjoy 'atmosphere'? We can create it at home too.

Noise

Noise is by far the most difficult aspect of our environment to control. The noise of traffic and the barking of neighbours' dogs are top of the list of environmental stresses.

The key factor in our reaction to noise is the amount of control we have over it. Research has shown that a person can endure a considerable degree of loud noise, so long as the sound can be switched off at will. The thought 'I can control this' keeps the stress at a low level of impact.

The second factor is the predictability of noise. The general hum of a ventilation system can be largely ignored. The intermittent banging of a hammer and the sporadic interruptions of a dog barking, sometimes furiously, sometimes plaintively, whining, growling, yapping, but apparently at random – these are stresses which are very difficult to forget.

It may be worth looking at what kind of noise we are suffering from and deciding on the best response.

- ***Loud predictable noise over which we have no control*** (e.g. an assembly line at a factory). Either we campaign to improve the working environment, change jobs or change our attitude to one of acceptance. The options are limited if we find our given work environment stressful and the compromise (like wearing earplugs) may have to be ours. Generally, though, noise that 'comes with the job' is not as severe a problem as noise that suddenly or persistently invades our domestic lives.
- ***Loud predictable noise over which we have some control.*** Faced with the rumble of heavy traffic outside our homes, what can we do? An occasional option is to change rooms around to create our main living area at the back of a property – a solution which is totally dependent on the size and structure of our home. There is another possibility. Just as we may organise a space, however tiny, for privacy, it may be worth considering making one room quieter than the others. Double-glazing is prohibitively expensive – but could *one* room be double-glazed? If we know that there is always somewhere to go which is at least a little quieter, it can help us to cope with the continual presence of noise. A bedroom or living room, furnished with plenty of soft material, acoustic tiles, even a double-door may be a very shrewd investment if such an expenditure is possible.

  If it is not, another alternative is to pay special attention to music in the home environment, counteracting negative sounds with positive. Restaurants often create calming, relaxing environments with sound as well as light, producing another 'world' which becomes – just off a noisy high street – a haven of enjoyment. Close attention to the quality of our whole environment – its cosiness and separateness from the pressures outside – may be a vital factor in being able to forget noise which we cannot obliterate.

- ***Unpredictable noise over which we feel we have no control.*** This is frequently the most stressful kind of noise, often originating from neighbours that we do not know or fear may be hostile to our requests for quiet. It can be beyond the wits of the calmest individual to cope with a dog, cruelly chained up all day, barking like crazy at the slightest sound in the street. But it is vital that we do take some control if we can.

  Writing a polite letter, if it is not possible to make a personal contact with a neighbour, can at least establish the idea of control in our minds. It also serves to let a person know that there is a problem – which is not always the case when endless late-night drilling is suffered in silence by a group of neighbours who 'don't want trouble' (but are getting plenty from the drill already). Our next step, perhaps with the support of several other residents, may be to bring in the Environmental Health Authorities. They do have statutory powers and can take action on our behalf. Recently, environmental health officers in Liverpool confiscated the hi-fi of a teenager after frequent complaints and warnings.

The point is to keep affirming the idea of some control over the problem, which can be achieved sooner or later: believing that we can do something, however long it takes, can alleviate some of our stress in the present moment. Feeling trapped and utterly overwhelmed will increasingly drive us to distraction.

Finally, controlling our hearing of the noise – with the use of earplugs – may be a temporary solution for an hour or so at night. But in the very worst predicaments it may be that relaxation exercises (see the next chapter) and any techniques we can adopt for changing our attitude to the problem may be the only relief which is immediately available.

Noise is a desperately difficult problem but our personal

survival, emotionally, is too important to allow others to dictate to us, whether it be an insensitive neighbour or an irresponsible council. Pneumatic drills at six o'clock on a Sunday morning, dogs, all-night parties, traffic – we need to find a way through this urban jungle.

Having said all that, there is something very tempting in the solution suggested in an advert which appeared in a local paper. It read:

F Mayhew and Sons. Funeral directors. Parties catered for.

Managing Type A behaviour

Noise is a clear case of a stressor that comes from the outside and we often feel very vulnerable to such environmental pressures. However, in the book *Type A Behaviour and Your Heart*, referred to earlier, the authors Friedman and Rosenmann concentrate on the stresses that arise from within. These are much more potent forces which we must take control over if we are to survive, whether emotionally or physically.

Friedman and Rosenmann offer a number of drills to counteract 'hurry-sickness', which they argue work for the Type A patients that are most in danger of serious heart disease. Among them are the following:

1 Try to restrain yourself from being the centre of attention by constantly talking. Make yourself listen to others. 'Begin in your professional [and personal] life to listen quietly to the conversation of other people. Quit trying to finish their sentences. An even better sort of drill for you if you have been in the habit of hastening the other person's speech rhythms is to seek out a person who stutters and then deliberately remain tranquil.'

2 'If you continue to need to talk unnecessarily, perhaps you ought to ask yourself the following questions: (1) Do I really have anything important to say? (2) Does anyone want to hear it? and (3) Is this the time to say it? If the answer to any one of these three questions is no, then remain quiet even if you find yourself biting your lips in frustration.'

3 Try to control your obsession with time by making yourself aware of it and changing your pattern of behaviour. For example, 'whenever you catch yourself speeding up your car in order to get through a yellow light at an intersection, penalise yourself by immediately turning to the right (or left) at the next corner. Circle the block and approach the same corner and [traffic] light again. After such penalisation you may find yourself racing a yellow light a second time, but probably not a third time.' You can help yourself in nearly all aspects of your life, including social situations, by seeking out opportunities to control your Type A behaviour. 'Purposely, with a companion, frequent restaurants and theatres where you know there will be a period of waiting. If your companion is your wife, remember that you spend far longer periods of time alone with her in your own home without fidgeting. If you and your companion cannot find enough to say to each other as you wait in a restaurant or a theatre, then you had both better seek different companions.'

4 In order to put some of your Type A behaviour into perspective, carry out a number of exercises. Develop periods of stillness and reflection in your self-created 'hectic programme for life', creating opportunities to assess the causes of your hurry sickness. One of the most important new habits to develop is a weekly review of the original causes of your present hurry sickness. Try to get to the heart of your problems and current obsessions. Is your time-dominated behaviour really a need to feel important? Is it designed to avoid some responsibility or person? Is it really essential to the success of your career or a particular goal? Friedman and Rosenmann offer this advice: 'Never forget when confronted by any task to ask yourself the following questions: (1) will this matter have importance five years from now? And (2) must I do this right now, or do I have enough time to think about the best way to accomplish it?'

5 Try to understand that the majority of your work and social life does not really require 'immediate action', but instead a worthwhile result in the long run or the gradual building up of a good relationship. 'Ask yourself, are good judgement and correct decisions best formulated under unhurried circumstances or under deadline pressures?'

6 Try to open up your life, broadening your aims. Take the steam out of the constant pressure of time which builds up inside you. Go to the theatre, read, sew. Give your attention to activities which require a different kind of involvement and a slower pace. Friedman and Rosenmann recommend that patients 'for drill purposes, attempt to read books that demand not only your entire attention but also a certain amount of patience. We have repeatedly advised our Type A patients to attempt reading Proust's eight-volume novel *The Remembrance of Things Past* not because it is one of the great modern classics (which it is) but because the author needs several chapters to describe an event that most Type A subjects would have handled in a sentence or two.'

7 Try not to make unnecessary appointments or deadlines. 'Remember, the more unnecessary deadlines you make for yourself, the worse your "hurry-sickness" becomes.'

8 Learn to protect your time. 'Try to never forget that if you fail to protect your allotment of time, no one else will. And the older you become, the more important this truth is.'

2 Working it Out

Two thousand, two hundred years ago, a man jumped out of a bath shouting, '*I've found it!*' He was not talking about the soap. He was talking about the solution to a complex scientific problem which had been bothering him for some time. His name was Archimedes and his joyful shout '*Eureka!*' has become proverbial.

Archimedes solved his problem of how to calculate volume by observing the displacement of water when he got into the tub. But there may be another reason why he solved it. Instead of pacing round his study, frowning and chewing his pencil – or biting his slate – he was relaxing.

Letting go

'My best ideas come to me in the bath' . . . if they do, and many make this claim, it is because the body is relaxed and the mind is free.

Relaxation is letting go. Letting go of the day, letting go of our worries. If stress draws us in, binds us, makes us 'uptight', relaxation frees us to be ourselves again: not a coiled spring or an overwound clock – but a person.

Body and mind are so closely connected that if we are anxious we become physically tense, but if we physically relax we can also reduce our anxiety. Relaxation exercises bring the parasympathetic branch of our nervous system into play. We calm down. The stress chemicals stop pumping into our system, alerting us for action – 'fight or flight'. Other biochemical reactions take place which produce feelings of tranquillity and rest. At our most completely relaxed, we fall asleep.

Sleep is the ultimate 'letting go' – and sleep disorders are often connected with our inability to do just that. Relaxation exercises, both physical and mental, help us to let go.

> 'I can't let go! I just can't – I've got so much on my mind! So much to do. So much to organise. So many responsibilities. There aren't enough hours in the day. Who wouldn't be worried with my life? Let go? Impossible!'

Impossible . . . like learning to swim. Learning to ride a bike. Seemingly impossible until, one day, we launch out on our own and just . . . let go.

Animals have no problem in relaxing. A dog can slump on the floor and freely let go of all activity. It can do this at will, many times a day. When there is a stimulus or a challenge, it will spring into action. But when nothing is happening, it collapses again in an enviable sprawl. A cat stretches itself with total abandonment. If only we could achieve that, but as we have already observed, humans anticipate problems, mull over the past, worry. Our minds keep chuntering along. We can't switch off. We just won't let go.

Sexual dysfunction can be caused by not being able to 'let go'. The experience of orgasm is the diametrical opposite of being in control. A woman who struggles desperately, hourly, to keep control, to hold her world together, may have difficulty in letting go when it comes to love-making. Equally, a man beset with worries may suffer from impotence. Therapy often involves relaxation exercises which teach people how to let go.

Our inability to let go, in the case of sexual or emotional problems, is not only a symptom of stress – it generates much more stress. Sexual dysfunction leads to great anxiety and distress in relationships. An emotionally 'uptight' person frequently over-reacts to almost every little crisis as if it were a major incident. The song 'Climb Every Mountain' could be adapted to 'Climb Every Molehill'. Everything becomes a drama and an effort and everybody is affected. If this is our case, then we need to take some advice from another well-worn cliché in the movies: 'Hey, just *loosen up*, will yer?'

There are many ways of loosening up and it is worth investing in a book devoted to the subject of relaxation (see recommendations in Books to Read). Relaxation tapes, with exercises and music, can be helpful too.

For the time being, choose some music which you find particularly soothing. An ideal example is 'Reverence' by Terry Oldfield. It combines the sounds of the natural world – the sea, whales, dolphins, the cry of gulls, with haunting flute music. Find something to suit your taste, but something gentle and atmospheric, not something dominating or too dramatic. Then, when you have time and privacy, try following these guidelines drawn up by Nita Catterton of the University of Virginia.

Deep relaxation technique

1 Sit in a comfortable position. (Support your upper back, neck, and head.) A quiet place where you will not be interrupted is best.

2 Slowly draw in and exhale a deep breath. Check your shoulders for stiffness or tense position. Allow them to fall naturally in a relaxed position. Take in a second deep breath and close your eyes.

3 Complete a body check to locate any areas of tension and tightness. Take each area and relax the muscles involved. Visualise the tension releasing and slipping away as warmth and relaxation flow into the area. You might imagine yourself basking in the sun and feeling the sun warm your area of tension. (If you are having difficulty evaluating whether or not you are relaxing a specific area try increasing the tension in that muscle and hold that tightness for a count of ten, then release.)

4 Starting with your feet, slowly work up through the body, relaxing muscle groups and areas of tightness and tension. Imagine warmth flowing into each area, muscles becoming heavy, and comforting relaxation replacing tightness or tension. Once you've progressed throughout your body, focus on your hands. (You can focus on any area of tension you'd like to work on.) Create a sentence that you can repeat to yourself emphasising warmth, heaviness, and relaxation, such as, 'My hands are warm, heavy, and relaxed.'

5 Do not be discouraged if at first your mind tends to wander away to other thoughts. Once you are aware that you have wandered to other thoughts simply come back and focus again on the area you are relaxing. Try to notice how good it feels to have some quiet time to yourself and how comfortable it is to let go of any tightness or tension you may have.

6 Deep relaxation is most effective when practised for a period of twenty minutes. If you find that sitting still for that long is more stress-inducing than stress-reducing, then start with a period of five or ten minutes and gradually build up to twenty minutes.

7 Always end your relaxation session with several deep breaths. Then, after slowly opening your eyes, maintain your relaxation position for a few minutes before resuming your next activity.

Make a commitment to practise deep relaxation on a daily basis for one month before determining if you want to continue with this stress-reduction technique.

Mental relaxation

A broad use of relaxation techniques covers our breathing, our muscles and our minds.

Mental relaxation can be invaluable, not only when we are 'uptight' or extremely anxious about something, but also in dealing with pain. The relationship between pain and relaxation is a telling example of how the mind and body interact. Toothache can torment us for days, but once we are sitting in the dentist's chair, it can go. We may be fearful of the drill but we are relieved that something is about to be done. Mental pressure eases and the pain subsides. The ability to relax mentally is a great advantage for women in labour, too. The more we struggle with pain rather than 'go with it', or let go, the worse it becomes. The same is certainly true of emotional pain which can be equally debilitating. How can we let go of the stressful thoughts that disturb our peace?

Dr Cary McCarthy offers this exercise as a way of evoking calm and relaxation.

Mental relaxation (five to ten minutes)

1. Select a comfortable position.
2. Close your eyes and think about a place that you have been before that represents your ideal place for physical and mental relaxation. (It should be a quiet environment, perhaps the seashore, the mountains, or even your own back garden. If you can't think of an ideal relaxation place, then create one in your mind.)
3. Now imagine that you are actually in your ideal relaxation place. Imagine that you are seeing all the colours, hearing the sounds, smelling the aromas. Just lie back, and enjoy your soothing, rejuvenating environment.
4. Feel the peacefulness, the calmness, and imagine your whole body and mind being renewed and refreshed.
5. After five to ten minutes, slowly open your eyes and stretch. You have the realisation that you may instantly return to your relaxation place whenever you desire, and experience a peacefulness and calmness in body and mind.

Animals know how to relax for very short periods – 'cat-napping' – and we need to relax often during the day too. The 'STOP' exercise has already been described. The religious equivalent is the 'arrow-prayer' – a momentary prayer. A few seconds of calm and collecting up strength to face a difficult situation. Relaxation can be like that, a few deep breaths, sitting still, eyes closed, head supported and relaxed, or standing up, but calm, silently repeating a phrase of reassurance: 'I have strength to cope', 'I am calm'.

Massage

One of the most effective ways of achieving relaxation is through massage. 'Massage parlours' are a popular subject for Sunday tabloids and are rapidly becoming part of comic folklore, which is why unfortunately some people can only think of touch in this way as sexual. But touch is vital to our emotional health and it is nothing less than a tragedy that our civilisation is so poverty-stricken when it comes to physical contact. Some individuals even shrink back from all touch, a hand on the shoulder, an arm round the waist, a kiss of greeting – because they cannot separate touch from sexual behaviour and to be touched, even by a close friend, makes them feel anxious and afraid. Massage can be sensual but it need not be sexual.

> 'Physically, massage relaxes you. It squeezes the tensions, the tightness, the toxins and the stress hormones out of the body – literally out of the muscles. The threat, the emergency, might have gone, but you have all those hormones still running round your body, still making you feel like you're under threat. So getting these things out of your body, getting them released, makes a huge difference.
>
> I think the trouble is that if people are chronically stressed it means that they have forgotten how to relax. It would be of no benefit to simply tell someone "You really need to relax". I think you have to give their body and their mind a real physical experience of what it feels like to be relaxed.'
>
> (Fiona Harrold, masseuse, from the TV series, *Relax*, BBC/Prospect Pictures, 1992)

To be massaged is to let go without fear and to be encouraged, soothed, into a state of relaxation. It can bond partners. It can be a family activity too, parent to child, child to parent. It can be male to male, female to female and between the sexes. Anyone can, in a loving and uncomplicated way, offer a massage to a friend in an environment free of ambiguity. A shoulder and neck massage can be given to a tense colleague in an office or to a nervous actor backstage. Friends down on the beach or at the swimming pool can give each other a massage to increase the enjoyment of relaxation. A massage can range from the art of the professional masseur, with lengthy skin to skin contact, in the context of a health club, all the way to the individual practice of 'self-massage' in private, at home or in the work environment.

Jane Madders in *Stress and Relaxation* gives these tips for self-massage:

> '***Self-massage***
>
> Don't think that because there is no one to give you a massage you must forgo all the benefits. There is a lot you can do yourself to help muscles relax and relieve discomfort. Electrical massage apparatus may help but some very simple massage using your own hands is effective.
>
> **Forehead**
>
> When you feel under strain, when your eyes are tired or when a headache is imminent, smooth out the worry muscles this way:
>
> Smooth gently from the centre outwards towards the temples.
>
> Smooth upwards towards the hair line one hand after the other.
>
> **Neck**
>
> When you have engaged in prolonged study or sedentary work, the muscles may prudently ache to warn you that it is time to give them a rest. [Jane Madders illustrates some neck exercises in her book, which can be followed by self-massage:]
>
> Let your head rest easily, not bent forward at all so that the muscles at the back are soft. Get hold of as much of the flesh as you can (it is rather like picking up a kitten by the scruff of its neck) then squeeze and let go several times.

With the tips of your fingers find the tender spots and press and let go with circular movements, without stretching the skin.

Shoulders
Many tense people have tender spots where the muscles join on to the shoulder blade. To relieve this, try to squeeze handfuls of the muscle and let go several times, then make pressing movements with your fingertips over the tender areas.

Legs
Give the large muscles of the thighs a shake with your hands. (You have probably seen football players and swimmers doing this to loosen up.) Then combine a kneading and squeezing movement of both hands, working alternately on each side of the thigh.

These are only a few self-massage techniques. You can adapt them for other parts of the body.'

Diet

Changing to a sensible diet can be an important element in reforming our whole lifestyle. It is vital to achieve a balance here as in all areas. A poor diet including too much sugar, caffeine, salt or alcohol, increases stress. But so too can an obsessive attitude about diet. Some people become so worried about the stressful effects of food additives on their children's behaviour, they will snatch an ice lolly away from a child as if it is sucking a stick of arsenic. They live in a state of tension in cafés, on holiday, at friends' houses, in fear of the world and all its evil additives. Perhaps wheeling their child around in an oxygen tent followed by an army of homeopaths is the only solution.

It is absurd to create stress in the effort to avoid it. Over-protective behaviour can be as damaging to a child's health as the wrong kind of orange juice. We should avoid harmful substances certainly, be sensible and where necessary strict in our diet, but we should not be neurotic. Natural foods should be complemented by natural behaviour. Of course, it is prudent to be very careful in the wake of public health crises – including BSE and the *E coli* outbreaks – but it is possible to do so without poisoning your children's imaginations with fears of living on a contaminated planet.

There are many very valuable guides to sensible eating and drinking and the use of food supplements, vitamin programmes, herbal and vegetarian cooking, ways of planning diets to reduce stress (see Books to Read). The best approach is to take an overview, looking in detail at this area of our life and initiate changes which are precise and consistent over many months.

Most of us should cut down on caffeine at the very least – if not cut it out. Caffeine has a short-term effect of 'mimicking' arousal, stimulating the heart and adrenal glands, but its side-effects are notorious – leading to headaches, exhaustion and irritability. Sugar, too, is a deceptive substance. It gives a temporary high, boosting energy, but in the long run it leads to greater tiredness. Adrenal glands are over-stimulated and become less effective at regulating blood sugar levels, which then drop further. Endless chocolate snacks can lead to . . . endless chocolate snacks. Compulsive eating, like drinking to relieve stress, creates its own damaging momentum of need, supply and greater need.

Physical exercise

Regular physical exercise increases our self-esteem. It has a beneficial effect on the way we feel about ourselves. It makes us look better and function more efficiently. It improves sleep patterns and can have a surprisingly deep impact on anxiety. It may not solve any problems but sometimes it can lift us when we feel low.

> 'Although exercise is tiring in itself physically, I find it quite energy-giving. I feel very refreshed afterwards. I sleep well

and I wake up really alert but the reason I don't exercise sometimes is because I'm so busy. I come home at the end of the day and it's nine o'clock at night. I've had a really long day and I'm too tired to go out and exercise, so then I wake up tired and sluggish. What I should really do is go to the gym and revitalise myself with some exercise but what I actually do is think I'm so tired I can't do it. So it's a vicious circle: if I don't exercise I just get tireder and tireder and tireder.'

(Jakki Brambles, disc jockey, from the TV series, *Relax*, BBC/ Prospect Pictures, 1992)

It is no coincidence that the best varieties of physical work-outs are those which involve more release and 'letting go' – cycling, swimming, jogging, aerobic dancing, rather than the more intense, striving activities of weight-lifting or doing push-ups. Aerobic exercise involves the whole body and, by the very nature and rhythm of these activities, the mind can achieve greater freedom.

Working out aggression

Working out in a gym, more than any other kind of exercise, may be valuable in dealing with the backlog of frustration and anger that builds up so easily inside us. No doubt many a punchbag – perhaps even thoughtfully provided by a corporation – has taken on the features of a hated employer. There is no getting away from it. Sometimes we just have to work out our anger physically. Theatres have 'crash boxes', old crates full of broken crockery, to make sound effects offstage. A domestic equivalent might not be a bad idea, where we could fling plates in a safe context . . .

Some people shut themselves in a bathroom and scream until they feel better, others find release in a strenuous activity like chopping wood or clearing undergrowth or digging a vegetable patch. Some people savagely scrub the floor or manically wash the car. Harmless, and organised, displacement of our anger can re-route our aggression and provide at least an emergency outlet.

This kind of homemade therapy is clearly very dependent on circumstances, to say the least. Competitive sport is arguably the classic way of dealing with pent-up aggression and 'socialising' our more destructive urges.

There is no doubt that anger needs to be released in physical ways and those who bottle it up for too long suffer harm. Mike Goldsmith, quoted in Part One, attributed his heart attack partly to a failure to express legitimate anger. However, our explosions of anger can hit the wrong target (literally in some cases) or create a serious escalation of stress, as we have seen in Part Two. We need to find more fundamental solutions. There is, undoubtedly, a time for 'going spare' in the bathroom or the garden shed, or working out in the gym alone, but ultimately it is hard to solve anything in the long term this way. We need to work through our anger and deal with our aggression more thoroughly (see Role Play and Assertiveness Training in the next chapter).

Meditation

Meditation conjures up images of Eastern mysticism for many. It's an alien philosophy, something to do with Buddhist monasteries or the lifestyle of ageing hippies chanting in their communes. We should abandon all such prejudices.

- Meditation can help anyone, in any situation.
- Meditation is a very simple form of mental relaxation which involves emptying the mind of all preoccupation in favour of one thought, image or word.
- Meditation focuses our mind, to the exclusion of all worries, in order to produce peace.
- Meditation need not be 'Transcendental Meditation' which is associated with a particular religious philosophy.
- Meditation can be profoundly Christian, as can be seen from the writings of the great mystics and saints, and it can be used to great benefit by Christians or by any religious faith without compromise.
- Meditation need not be religious at all.

Meditation can be as simple as sitting in a quiet room, in a comfortable position, breathing deeply through the nose, relaxing, and then choosing a word or an image. The word may be meaningful or not. It might simply be the number 'one', which we repeat over and over again, following the rhythm of our breathing.

Breathe in and out and then repeat 'one'. Do this for several minutes. Focus on the word 'one' to the exclusion of everything else. Or we might choose a word like 'water'. We focus on the word, repeat it, allowing our mind to explore the idea of water – a running river, tap water, a child in the womb, the sea – but always bringing our thoughts back to the word 'water'. All other thoughts and words are excluded except this one element in our lives: 'water'.

Another kind of meditation is visual. We can light a candle. Watch the flame. It's an ancient, timeless image. It can comfort. It can inspire. 'Light'. Perhaps we are in a dark situation and need light to see our way through. Meditation for twenty minutes, perhaps daily for a while, can focus our minds on light, an image which returns when dark thoughts cloud our lives.

Visualisation

Visualisation is another practice, close to meditation, which is sometimes used in alternative treatments for cancer or by psychotherapists to help their patients.

- Visualise a blackboard. Visualise yourself writing all your worries on that board, all the things bothering you now. Fill the board. Now imagine yourself holding a damp cloth. Wipe that cloth slowly across the board. Wipe out the problems one by one.
- Visualise a rubbish skip. Visualise yourself taking all the junk from your past, all the mistakes and the hurts. Tip them into the skip. Now visualise the lorry that comes to hook up the skip and take it away for ever.
- Visualise the adult who is causing you the most trouble as a

six-year-old. Imagine them playing in the street. See them as they once were, lovely and carefree, before being moulded by life into such a harsh personality. Picture them being hurt by the violent quarrelling of their parents or by some other terrible stress in their life. Imagine yourself comforting, rather than hating, them.

These are just some simple ways of gaining greater perspective on our lives, but one of the deepest ways of restoring harmony is to turn to nature.

Taking our worries for a walk

Many of us are afraid of 'wasting time', but often it is not time that is being wasted but us. 'Getting and spending we lay waste our powers' – Wordsworth's warning, written in London nearly two hundred years ago, has not been heeded. When we contemplate the mystery of nature, we can act to restore our sanity.

Looking at forces outside ourselves and seeing rhythms that are indifferent to our own ups and downs can be very soothing. The changing seasons, the ebb and flow of the tide, the immense power of the summer sun setting in all its glory – here is a power which can calm and inspire.

Often we are dying emotionally when all around us life pushes its way up from the barren earth. The growth of a bulb in a plant pot, the arrival of a solitary snowdrop, can be a reminder of hidden forces within ourselves. These can be images for meditation too – not some kind of bizarre chanting or weird religious ritual or romantic self-indulgence – but images of normality on which we can focus our minds in times of greatest stress and difficulty.

A sense of wonder at nature is one of the most precious gifts. Children have it instinctively. A small detail, a tadpole in a pond or a curled-up autumn leaf on a pavement will fascinate a two-year-old, and yet we will crunch through piles of leaves and stalk past a pond teeming with life, lost in our own thoughts and problems. And this mental self-absorption becomes our only activity. We are our only subject-matter.

Sometimes an image from nature can be the beginning of a new hope, a release from the prison of our minds. The poet Irina Ratushinskaya, who experienced literal imprisonment in a Soviet labour camp, wrote a poem called 'I will live and survive'. She gives an answer to anyone who asks how she has survived the appalling suffering:

> And I'll be asked: what helped us to live
> When there were neither letters nor any news – only walls,
> And the cold of the cell, and the blather of official lies,
> And the sickening promises made in exchange for betrayal.
> And I will tell of the first beauty
> I saw in captivity.
> A frost-covered window! No spyholes, nor walls,
> Nor cell-bars, nor the long-endured pain –
> Only a blue radiance on a tiny pane of glass,
> A cast pattern – none more beautiful could be dreamt!
> The more clearly you looked, the more powerfully blossomed
> Those brigand forests, campfires and birds!
> And how many times there was bitter cold weather
> And how many windows sparkled after that one –
> But never was it repeated,
> That upheaval of rainbow ice!
> And anyway, what good would it be to me now,
> And what would be the pretext for that festival?
> Such a gift can only be received once,
> And perhaps it is only needed once.
> (*No, I'm Not Afraid*, poems by Irina Ratushinskaya translated by David McDuff)

'I lost my son, I lost my granddaughter, I lost my best friend, I lost my brother-in-law, all in a matter of three years and it was an extremely stressful period for me. I got involved in gardening which I never ever did before. I mean, I used to mow the lawns and that was my lot. But when I lost my son and then my granddaughter, I found that going into the garden and working in the garden, weeding and seeding and growing my own plants was a great relief. A great relief. I found that I was always thinking about Mark, but I'd find that I'd see a weed and for a few seconds, I wouldn't think about Mark. Then for another few seconds I wouldn't think about Mark because I was absolutely concentrating on what I was doing and it was a tremendous help for me.

The way that I found that I got rid of a lot of tension was that I used to go into the garden on my own. I used to go down to the back of the garden and I would sit there and collapse sometimes. I would cry and I would cry. Oh God, I would cry! It released a lot of tension for me and I can do that now. I can go out tonight and when I get built up inside I go down there and I do a lot of crying.'

(Mike Reid, actor in *EastEnders*, from the TV series, *Relax*, BBC/Prospect Pictures, 1992)

We don't need to be poets or natural historians like David Bellamy, or astronomers like Carl Sagan, to have some appreciation of the world beyond our own brains. Yet, when we turn outwards, it is usually to people rather than to the natural world. This is right and natural in itself, but sometimes it is impossible to find joy in the relationships that have become the greatest source of our stress. At such times our joy may need to come from other sources, from deep and ancient springs. We are frequently reminded that we must not neglect the heritage of our earth, but this is not just a general, political issue. It is personal. There may be those who ardently campaign for the rainforests but become so busy, tense and irritable as they overload themselves with work in their noble cause that they cannot find time to enjoy a raindrop falling down a window or appreciate the tree that grows silently and mysteriously in their own back garden.

Nature offers us its glorious inspiration for free. Some advice in 'self-help' articles or books depends on resources we may not have – in particular, money. Most of us can't get back to nature by selling our £300,000 house in the suburbs and buying a farm in France. Nor can we afford expensive holidays – perhaps we get no holiday away from our environment at all. Sometimes we are absolutely stuck where we are. We may have no resources whatsoever, no possibility of *ever* moving from the high-rise building that we're living in – or it certainly seems like that. But even in the most derelict areas of a city there are often, in the rubble and on the wastegrounds, signs of life. Even in the most desperate situations there can be snow on a window-box or the song of a skylark ascending on a summer evening. Joy in the smallest things is not some kind of 'Sound of Music' philosophy, a soppy substitute for environmental and social action (see the chapter 'Power and Responsibility') – it is an essential part of our spiritual survival kit when things seem utterly impossible.

The French novelist André Gide said, 'Without worship, we shrink.' If we have no sense of anything beyond ourselves and our own problems, however desperate, then we do shrink. Like Alice in Wonderland, gradually everything seems to tower over us. Our fears become outsize. Nature can help to restore our perspective at such times. It can help to take our worries for a walk.

Building a playroom

Imagine if the human being were represented as a house. Most of us would have a large kitchen. We do plenty of eating. We'd have a large study or workshop, considering the hours we spend at work, or a vast broom-cupboard in proportion to the chores we do each day. There would be a reasonable bedroom. Time for some sleep and sex, maybe. But only the tiniest bathroom. Hardly any time for real physical relaxation. There'd be no garden for some of us – we ignore nature too much of the time. And there would definitely be no playroom. Maybe a box of toys somewhere in a corner, but no room. No real area for play-time in the brain.

But play, whether it's music, leisure activities, hobbies, theatre-going, sports matches, parties, or 'just having a laugh' is a vital part of our human identity. It is also one of our greatest weapons against stress. An ancient Hebrew writer described wisdom as 'ever at play in the world'. It is truly wise to have fun.

To have fun, in the deepest sense, is to live creatively. It means making the most of our gifts or the gifts of others. Music is so important an influence on our lives, yet it is often debased – meaningless muzak in lifts, half-heard pop songs infiltrating our minds from somebody else's blaring radio, a melody lost in the frenetic imagery of a three-minute video. It is good to spend time with music, without pictures, wholly devoted to the experience. Time to listen. Time to lose ourselves in the power and beauty or strangeness of a classical composition or the excitement and subtlety of jazz or the dynamism of a rock album.

We need time and variety in our fun – but perhaps the most vital ingredient of all in 'play' is a sense of humour. Woody Allen said: 'Most of the time I don't have much fun. The rest of the time, I don't have any fun at all.' That is worryingly true of many people. There is even such a thing now as 'laughter therapy', using 'laughter exercises' to reduce tension. That idea somehow has the ring of a very humourless civilisation. But we do need to apply 'laughter therapy' to ourselves.

The quality of much of our lives, and our ability to survive the worst situations, may depend upon the answer we give to these three questions:

- How seriously do you take life?
- Can you laugh at yourself?
- Do you see the funny side of things, even in a crisis?

> 'I had an aunt I loved very, very dearly. I adored her. She died young – she was only 45 – and that was stressful, that was painful, it hurt. Her mother, my grandmother, had died only a year earlier, but she being a grandmother was an older person. I was devastated by my aunt's death and someone said to me at the funeral, "Thank God your grandmother

> didn't live to see this day. It would have killed her!" It was wonderful because it was funny and I thought she would have liked that joke. My aunt would have loved it and I felt better. Yes, being able to laugh at even the worst things does help enormously.'
>
> (Claire Rayner, writer and broadcaster, from the TV series, *Relax*, BBC/Prospect Pictures, 1992)

The therapeutic value of humour cannot be overestimated. Thankfully, we have the richest comic tradition in Britain. Basil Fawlty, frantically beating his car with the branch of a tree because it won't start, makes us laugh at ourselves. National self-mockery is probably far more important for national survival than any 'stiff-upper-lip' attitude to a crisis.

Laughter, like nature, brings perspective. Even better than time, it can help to heal our wounds.

3 Talking it Out

Talking to ourselves is popularly described as 'the first sign of madness', but it can be invaluable. We need to learn to have our own 'mental monologues', to ask questions of ourselves and give honest answers. We often have positive and negative thoughts jostling around in our heads when we are faced with worries and problems. We can use these dynamically.

The stress experts J C Quick and J D Quick have produced the following chart which illustrates how constructive self-talk can operate in many situations.

Situation	***Typical Mental Monologue***	***Constructive Self-talk Alternative***
Driving to work on a day which you know will be full of appointments and potentially stressful meetings.	'Oh boy, what a day this will be!' 'It's going to be hell.' 'I'll never get it all done.' 'It'll be exhausting.'	'This looks like a busy day.' 'The day should be very productive.' 'I'll get a lot accomplished today.' 'I'll earn a good night's rest today.'
Anticipation of a seminar presentation or public address.	'What if I blow it?' 'Nobody will laugh at my opening joke.' 'What if they ask about . . . ?' 'I hate talking to groups.'	'This ought to be a challenge.' 'I'll take a deep breath and relax.' 'They'll enjoy it.' 'Each presentation goes a bit better.'
Recovering from a heart attack.	'I almost died. I'll die soon.'	'I didn't die. I made it through.'

Situation	***Typical Mental Monologue***	***Constructive Self-talk Alternative***
	'I'll never be able to work again.' 'I'll never be able to play sports again.'	'The doctor says I'll be able to get back to work soon.' 'I can keep active and gradually get back to most of my old sports.'
Difficulty with a superior at work.	'I hate that person.' 'He makes me feel stupid.' 'We'll never get along.'	'I don't feel comfortable with him.' 'I let myself get on edge when he's around.' 'It will take some effort to get along.'
Flat tyre on a business trip.	'Damn this old car.' (Paces around car, looking at flat tyre.) 'I'll miss all my meetings.' 'It's hopeless.'	'Bad time for a flat.' (Begins to get tools out to start working.) 'I'll call and cancel Jenkins at the next phone. I should make the rest of the appointments.'

J C Quick and J D Quick, *Organizational Stress and Preventive Management* (New York: McGraw-Hill, 1984).

There are many ways this technique can be developed. Faced with a worrying thought like 'I'm going to be late', we can sometimes defuse it by repeatedly asking ourselves: 'What then?'

The 'What then?' Exercise

'This train is going to be an hour late.'
'What then?'
'I'll have to rush for a taxi.'

'What then?'

'I'll get stuck in traffic.'

'What then?'

'I'll arrive half an hour late for the meeting, sweating all over.'

'What then?'

'I'll apologise to everyone and explain what happened.'

'What then?'

'If we don't finish all the business, we'll have to fix another meeting.'

'What then?'

'I'll collapse in my chair, at my desk, utterly exhausted. A wasted day.'

'What then?'

'Then . . . there's tomorrow . . .'

The object of this exercise is to put our worry into perspective. What am I afraid of? What is the worst scenario here? Is it that bad? *Fretting over being late* is how the day is being wasted, even more than being late. Now the worry is controlled, how about using the delay creatively? Sleep, meditation, the enjoyment of the view, conversation, planning ahead, thoughts of holidays, writing a letter . . . the day can be rescued.

Writing memos to ourselves

Sometimes it may be helpful to write thoughts down. Faced with a troubling situation that haunts us, or a worry that dogs us persistently, writing can be a kind of exorcism. Once down on paper, perhaps with good and bad aspects of the problem listed in columns, our worry can be managed. It is taken out of the twilight world of the 'back of our minds' into broad daylight. 'Here's my problem. Let's have a good look at it.'

Lists of pros and cons are often used by people when making difficult decisions. Other lists could be invented too. In chapter 1, disappointment was included as one of the most stressful elements in life. Looking at forthcoming events, we can train ourselves to be realistic.

First, write down a few examples of disappointment in the past. Then choose the next two or three most important future events in your life. Compare your expectations with the probable reality.

The daydreamer's guide to reality

	Age	Event	Expectation	Reality
PAST	7	Christmas	Wonderful time	Got flu
	14	First date	Kissing in the Tunnel of Love	She cancelled
	18	Driving test	Sail through – no problem	Failed
	21	First job	Exciting challenge	Frustration
FUTURE		Marriage	Ideal partnership	Rewarding but needs hard work too, learning to be unselfish
		Having a baby	Perfect child	Exciting but tiring, changes life for everyone, love and patience needed
		Moving house	A nicer property in a better area – a happier life	May have some disadvantages too, takes time to make new friends, good idea to move but allow for readjustment
		Starting a new business	Success, making a fortune, independence	Total dedication needed, new demands on the family – may be hard times ahead, stick at it, success takes time and courage

One advantage of this exercise is that experience may well prove to be much better than the sober 'realistic' estimate we have written down. We can be surprised by our good fortune rather than constantly let down by life.

'Mental monologues' or 'Memos to ourselves' are really ways of increasing control and, in this way, boosting our self-esteem. Negative voices within do so much harm. 'You can't cope', 'You're a failure', 'There you go again – making a fool of yourself'. We need to give ourselves a much higher score in life. 'That was good', 'That was an improvement on last time', 'Surprising what you can manage', 'Well done!' This isn't self-indulgence. It is life-saving. A low self-image – invariably a false image – sinks us into a deep well of self-hatred and despair that some people never come up from. But there is always a way up. Encouragement is the elixir of life to a little child – 'Well done! Go on, you can do it!' Even as adults, we need to keep taking the medicine.

Judging ourselves

The trouble is, we often live our lives as if our decisions could be judged by a mathematical model of correctness. There is one *right* decision but an infinite number of *wrong* ones. This gives us limitless capacity for being wrong and overwhelming odds against being right. Consequently, we feel crushed by failure much of the time.

If we must make judgements about our lives, it is vital that they are not simply of the right–wrong/success–fail/win–lose type. Thinking like this, we write ourselves off: 'I've blown it', 'Failed again', 'What an idiot'. Equally, the arrogant blindness of someone who always says, 'I'm right', 'I never make mistakes' is an absurdity.

Often, we need to make value judgements which involve many different shades. Faced with the stress of feeling we have made a 'wrong' decision about something, which may well have nothing to do with questions of morality or legality but simply be a decision to leave a job or take out a second mortgage, we can helpfully review the situation on paper.

Draw a scale of 'degrees of good sense'. It might look like this:

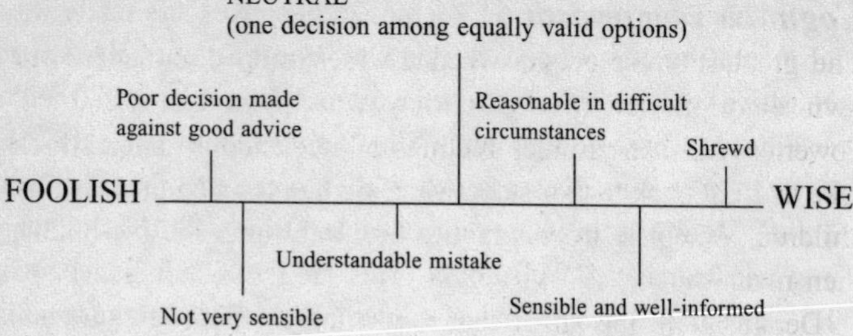

If we take the opposite poles of the scale, ranging from the feeling 'I am a complete moron' to the conviction 'I am a genius with divine illumination', we could say that most of our decisions lie well between these two extremes. Very many of our 'worst failures', in fact, hover round the middle.

Scales like this can be used to establish perspective: a reasonable assessment of ourselves is always an investment in dealing with stress. People try to push us to extremes – 'It's all your fault.' Or we accept their judgements too readily, anticipating blame by admitting, 'It's all my fault,' and then thinking despairingly, 'It's always my fault – I'm the problem here.' We need to sort out clearly what *is* our problem and what, in fact, is nothing to do with us at all. Again, a scale can clarify our thoughts:

It's all my fault ———————— Everyone else is to blame

If we view the problem at either end of this scale, we will often create unnecessary stress. It may be true that something is genuinely 'all my fault' or 'all somebody else's'. This is sometimes the case. But not always. Rarely are the extremes true in the complex of human relationships.

It is helpful to have our own assessment of responsibility, in order to counter those who try to blame us for everything. To be able to say, 'Yes, I agree with this but I don't accept that.'

Cognitive reappraisal

The greatest stress occurs when we feel trapped, either by our own emotions or in a situation which we can't control. Powerlessness can produce feelings of tremendous anger, which take us right back to that stage when we had least control, as tiny children. We suffer from infantile rage, tantrums – if not bodily, then mentally.

Dealing with the anger that rages in our minds, like a consuming forest fire sparked off by a small incident, is one of the most difficult tasks. Difficult but critical to survival. 'Cognitive reappraisal' is a term for learning to think about situations differently. It means discovering that we are not trapped but we do have options. There are various ways in which we can react. We have choices to make, every day of our lives.

Supposing a workmate, who is known to fiddle the books and cheat his employers, is given promotion and you are passed over. Which reaction do you choose?

Headbanger

Furious anger at being treated this way. Take it out on others.

Pragmatist

Accept that this is a painful fact of life. Get on with your work.

Reformer

Campaign for better decision-making in the firm, involving consultation at shop-floor level where there is better knowledge of the workforce. Discuss your concerns in confidence with respected peers.

Alchemist

Turn base metal into gold. Decide to turn this bad experience to good in any way possible. Equip yourself to cope when things don't go your way or even get worse. Make an informed decision to stay and be positive – or leave.

All of these reactions are possible options, or we might pass through them all in stages over a period of months – but to get stuck in the first option and never move on is a disastrous course of action.

Anger takes us over. It suddenly overwhelms us. It is extremely easy to forget that it is also a choice. We cannot prevent ourselves from feeling angry or hurt: but we can decide whether to stay angry or stay hurt. If we continually choose the negative option, all our relationships will be affected.

> Two women joined a firm of accountants at the same time. On the first day, one of the women went up to the old secretary and whispered, 'What are the people like in this firm?' The secretary asked her, 'What were they like in the office where you worked before?' 'Oh, terrible.' 'Well in that case,' replied the secretary, 'they're terrible here as well.' Later, the second newcomer asked the secretary the same question. Again she asked, 'What were they like in your last office?' 'Oh very nice.' 'Well then,' she smiled, 'in that case, they're very nice here too.'

How much 'baggage' we carry from the past can determine how light our journey will be into the future. If we carry the weight of our destructive attitudes or insecurities, we will blight relationships wherever we go.

But how do we go about changing our feelings about life, in particular deep emotions like anger and grief which must be expressed very openly and honestly? There are certainly no easy answers, no slick solutions to what has to be a slow transformation. Certainly we must not deny but pour out our heartbreak and our anguish, our rage and frustration, in many situations. But when these emotions become an end in themselves, when we get stuck, we start to deny the options. Eventually we come to live a half-life, where 'nothing ever changes'.

How can we change? Cognitive reappraisal is about wanting to change, to think differently about ourselves and our circumstances. The way forward means a determination to take responsibility, at least for our own lives. The rest of this chapter looks at this challenge, but cognitive therapy is also discussed in 'A Problem Shared' (page 203).

Negative capability

In the second part of this book, we looked at numerous 'poor coping strategies'. One of the more subtle, and generally hidden, attitudes of mind is our tendency to romanticise our lives. Cognitive reappraisal will inevitably lead us to be more realistic and pragmatic, less vulnerable to wild optimism. One of the greatest 'romantic poets' coined a phrase which is the true antidote to shallow romanticism. John Keats spoke of great art being characterised by 'negative capability', and he defined this as the ability to hold contrary forces in tension 'without any irritable reaching out for fact and reason'. The human being who can live with contradictions and questions is ultimately much deeper and richer than the person who sees everything in simplistic terms. If we accept a person's faults realistically, yet see their potential and their strengths, we will love them more profoundly. If we evaluate a business relationship accurately and live with the minuses as well as the pluses, we will make strong partnerships. If we can live through doubts and periods of simply not knowing the answers, we will escape dogmatism and find a deeper religious faith. Above all, if we refuse to romanticise ourselves in our own eyes, accepting our own shortcomings and weaknesses, paradoxically we are much more likely to change for the better and become stronger.

Act as you will become

One striking way of changing for the better was adopted by the actor Anthony Hopkins. He was forced to face inner contradictions and struggles through the blight of alcoholism on his life. He spoke of his struggle in an interview with the psychiatrist Anthony

Clare on BBC Radio 4. In some of the major changes of his life he had adopted the Shakespearian advice, 'Assume a virtue if you have it not.' The advice to 'act as you will become' was given by the psychologist William James one hundred years ago.

To illustrate this, think of attending a job interview. You may not feel confident, but the decision to 'act as if you are confident' is a significant choice. It is not deceiving anyone but a way of learning a new role. Initially, there may well be tension between what you feel about yourself and the image you present to a prospective employer. But confidence breeds confidence. Her confidence in you, for example, may well inspire changes in your self-image.

This is no modern gimmick. Jewish culture has understood this for centuries. In the synagogue, those who are mourning – still feeling terrible grief and sadness – are given a special prayer to say together: the Kaddish. It is a prayer of praise and thanksgiving. The act of saying this regularly is part of the cleansing of the emotions and the healing. 'Act as you will become' . . .

Psycho-drama and role-play

This is one of the reasons why psycho-drama and role-play can be so valuable. A person who has great difficulty 'letting go', who cannot – perhaps for very good reasons – trust others is encouraged to do 'trust exercises' (although these should be carefully supervised).

A simple trust exercise is to stand, eyes closed, between two people with their arms outstretched. At first the 'supporters' stand very close, one supporting your back, the other your front. Gradually, as you fall a few inches forwards, then backwards, they move a little further apart, supporting you all the time but increasing the level of trust. You fall backwards but you are held and gently pushed forwards. Again you are held. You are completely safe and can relax. You learn to depend on your partners. A much more advanced trust exercise is to fall backwards off a table into a tunnel of people who are gripping each other's hands and making a bed to catch you. This is a very simple, utterly reliable and well-nigh impossible exercise for many adults to do. Children find it much easier. In most cases, they have not yet lost their ability to trust.

Gradually moving towards greater trust, through simple exercises, can have a very deep impact on the emotions. Playing out 'trust' can move slowly towards 'becoming trusting'. Often self-help groups (see the next chapter) adopt these techniques for building confidence. Encounter groups exist in many parts of Britain which explore relationships through psycho-drama and role-play.

Anger, as we have seen, is one of the most intractable of emotions. How do we act calm? Most of us try to do just that at great cost – we suppress our emotions and make anger worse. In no way should we ever hide or fail to deal with our anger. But there are ways that role-play can help, sometimes very profoundly, allowing us to express anger but also converting it to good use.

There is no mystique about role-play. It is simply using the principle behind the imaginative play of children, party games like charades or improvisation exercises in the theatre to deepen our understanding of ourselves and our relationships. Psychotherapists sometimes use role-play with patients. One of the most famous exercises is the 'empty chair' developed by Fritz Perls in Gestalt Therapy. A person talks to a chair as if someone they know is sitting there. Unresolved feelings such as anger and grief can be expressed – but the person in therapy then sits on the chair and takes on the role of the absent character, imagining how they would reply and what they would feel.

Role-play can often be a helpful release when it is impossible to deal with a relationship directly (the person who has hurt us in the past may be dead or beyond our reach). However, deep solutions may only come by facing up to the relationship itself and dealing with the source of our stress openly and fairly. In the case of 'talking out' problems in the context of a potential confrontation, it is vital that our behaviour is neither aggressive nor passive. Both of these options increase stress. The aim is to deal with it.

Assertiveness training

Learning to be assertive is to acknowledge your own rights and the rights of others. To be non-assertive, passive or repressive, is to deny your own rights. To be aggressive, however, is to deny the rights of others. Psychologist Sandra Langrish gives a very good illustration of this.

> 'Imagine, for example, you are working on a project. It is 4.30 p.m. and you have arranged to meet a friend at 5.00 p.m. so that you can go for a meal and a theatre visit together. Your boss rushes into your office waving a piece of paper. He has just received a telephone call about some aspect of the project which requires the preparation of an additional document, ". . . right now!" You realise it will take until at least 5.45 to do the work. What do you say?
>
> *Non-assertive response*: "That's OK. I'll drop what I'm doing and do it right now. Just leave it with me. I'll take care of it."
>
> *Aggressive response*: "What do you take me for? Do you think I've got nothing better to do than jump when you whistle? Well, if you do, you've got a big shock coming! I'm going out with a friend, and I'm leaving at 5.00 on the dot. Just find someone else to run after you."
>
> *Assertive response*: "I realise that it's important that this is done as soon as possible but I've made arrangements to meet a friend at 5.00 p.m., so I can't do it now. However, I'll do it first thing tomorrow." '

Assertiveness training can be invaluable and courses are generally available nationwide. Local libraries or adult education centres can provide details. The structure will vary but will usually include some drama and role-play as part of the training. It is worth noting that role-play need not be intense at all and can be great fun, even hilarious, in a lively group – where good friendships can be formed, too.

Assertiveness skills are of two main kinds, verbal and non-verbal. Again, Sandra Langrish illustrates what it means to be assertive.

> ‘When being *assertive*, a person generally establishes good eye contact, stands or sits comfortably without fidgeting and talks in a strong, steady voice, neither shouting nor mumbling. Assertive words include “I” statements such as “I think”, “I feel”, “I want”; cooperative words such as “let's”, or “we could”, and empathic statements of interest such as “what do you think”, “how do you feel”.
>
> A *non-assertive* response is self-effacing and may be accompanied by such mannerisms as the shifting of weight, downcast eyes, a slumped body posture or a hesitant, giggly or whining voice. Non-assertive words can include qualifiers such as “maybe”, “I wonder if you could”, “only”, “just”, “would you mind very much”, “I can't”, or fillers such as “you know”, “well”, “uh”, and negators: “it's not really important”, “it's all right”, “don't bother”.
>
> An *aggressive* response is typically expressed by inappropriate anger or hostility which is loudly and explosively uttered. It is characterised by glaring eyes, leaning forward or pointing a finger, and an angry tone of voice. Aggressive words include threats such as “you'd better” or “if you don't watch out”, put-downs such as “come on”, or “you must be kidding”, and evaluative comments such as “should”, “I thought you'd know better”. Indirectly aggressive behaviour uses the language of the non-assertive response combined with the non-verbal behaviour of the aggressive mode, concentrating on body posture and angry movements.’

Learning to deal with difficult relationships is an enviable skill. It is hard won. But learning to ‘be ourselves’, whatever the pressure on us, can drastically reduce our stress load.

> ‘Some people are naturally assertive because they've had all their needs met as a child. But it's harder if you've had to battle in life. In school you may have had a teacher who labelled you as clumsy or stupid or dumb. We actually believe these things that are said to us, the label given to

us. In doing that we lose our confidence, our inner confidence. We may be great at our job but totally inadequate at dealing with other people. Assertive training empowers you to recognise your own needs and to state those needs clearly without blaming the other person. In doing that you have a happier lifestyle and you are capable of dealing with the stress in your life.'

(Bridget Tracey, assertiveness trainer, from the TV series, *Relax*, BBC/Prospect Pictures, 1992)

Handling the 'stress-makers'

Most of us are agents of stress in the lives of others, so there is no room for complacency. In looking at a classic 'stress-maker' – the manipulator – we may need to check our own behaviour too. Manipulators have many techniques from flattery, 'You're the only person who can do this' ('I want you to work overtime'), to guilt, 'You won't let me down, will you?' ('I have a right to exploit your good nature'). Sometimes a manipulator will use subtle techniques to rouse us to anger on their behalf, artfully sowing seeds of their own destructive emotions into our unsuspecting minds: 'I don't want this to upset you, but . . .'

One way of dealing with all forms of manipulation is to form mental sub-titles. Every time someone tries to manipulate you verbally, sub-title their words:

- *'After all I've done for you'*
  ('Do what I say or else')
- *'You people are always creating extra work for me'*
  ('I've got pressures at home and I'm not coping at the moment')
- *'Really, I don't mind'*
  ('Really, I do mind')

Clearly, the better you know someone, the more likely you are to guess the 'sub-text' accurately. It may help you to be compassionate at times, but above all fair, firm and assertive in dealing with all the 'martyrs', 'flatterers', 'bullies' and other species of manipulator.

One further technique can be used for dealing with persistent pressure from a colleague or relative, perhaps over many years. This is to catalogue and number their characteristic remarks. A boss who says, for the fiftieth time, 'I'm counting on you to co-operate' is using remark 5. If he says, 'I've given you a chance with this job – so don't blow it,' he's using number 8. These are among his numerous techniques for making you do whatever he wants, fair or unfair. If a mother says to a grown-up child, 'I can see you're not coping again,' she's using number 14, a well-worn device for making sure her son or daughter never learns to cope without her. The 'numbers game' is a useful mental blocking device. 'Here we go again. Number 3!' It need not be harsh but a good-humoured, internal method of handling manipulators. In this way, we can still remain loyal and hard-working, affectionate and dutiful – but not become putty in the manipulator's hands at any cost.

The stress diary

Progress can be slow in learning to handle old relationships in a new way, but progress there must be. One way of challenging ourselves to move on is to keep a stress diary (see overleaf). We can chart the upsets in our lives over a period of time and see how we are learning to face them.

The art of communication

So much of our trouble in life comes down to the art of communication. We need to hone our tools of language and of behaviour finely. We need to perfect the art of listening as well as talking, interpreting messages clearly from others, even when scrambled or hidden. We need to understand what the other person is saying, with patience and insight wherever possible – even when they are being unfair. But, above all, we need to make our own position clear.

Date		*Incident*	*People involved*
Week 1	Monday		
	Tuesday		
	Wednesday		
	Thursday		
	Friday		
	Saturday		
	Sunday		
Week 2	Monday		
	Tuesday		
	Wednesday		
	Thursday		
	Friday		
	Saturday		
	Sunday		
Week 3	Monday		
	Tuesday		
	Wednesday		
	Thursday		
	Friday		
	Saturday		
	Sunday		
Week 4	Monday		
	Tuesday		
	Wednesday		
	Thursday		
	Friday		
	Saturday		
	Sunday		

What you did	***What you should have done***

- Speak clearly.
- Say everything you need to say. Don't deliver confusing half-messages: 'I'm not terribly happy about this but don't let's bother about that now.' Explain why you aren't happy, simply and reasonably.
- Be specific. Don't generalise. 'People will have trouble with this.' Which people? What trouble?
- Communicate the same message non-verbally as well as verbally. Don't say, 'That's completely fine by me,' whilst furrowing your brow and biting your nails.
- Listen carefully and be actively involved. Don't mind-read, fill in what the other person is trying to say or make assumptions.
- Check out with the other person: explain what you think they have said and make sure that you both have the same understanding.
- Keep the communication going until you both have the same idea of what has been said. Whether agreeing, disagreeing, instructing or collaborating, it is important to have a common bond of understanding even if that means, 'We agree on what we disagree about.'

(These guidelines are freely adapted from seven points on communication first suggested by Martin Shaffer in the book *Life after Stress*.)

Good communication is so vital in every area of life and it is most vulnerable in those situations where we desperately want to hear the opposite of what is being said. Unrequited love is the most painful example of this. The person desperate to be loved, seizes on the tiniest scrap of encouragement and blows it up to massive proportions. 'She said that she wouldn't object too much if I rang her again' becomes very quickly 'She wants me to ring her', which graduates to 'I'm sure she fancies me'.

It is extremely hard to communicate clearly in such situations. But sometimes, to deal with extreme stress, it is very necessary.

The most difficult person of all is the one who 'won't take "no" for an answer'. Yet that is sometimes because we don't *give* 'no' for an answer.

The two simplest and most difficult words of all to say, in any language, are 'yes' and 'no'. The secret of knowing when – and how – to say these two words clearly is also the secret of gaining much greater control over our lives.

To learn, above all, to say 'no', lovingly, firmly, repeatedly, clearly, is to take a great deal of stress away from our diaries and our relationships. To be able to say 'no' is often to be able to say 'yes' to peace.

4 A Problem Shared

The 1960s was a decade when the idea of 'community' was in vogue. There were communes and cults, collectives and co-operatives, there were love-ins, 'togetherness', encounter groups, touch therapy, there was 'wholeness' and 'oneness'. It was a decade of sharing and caring. It was also a decade of loneliness.

> Eleanor Rigby died in the church and was buried along with her name.
> Nobody came.
> Father McKenzie, wiping the dirt from his hands as he walks from the grave.
> No one was saved.
> All the lonely people, where do they all come from?
> All the lonely people, where do they all belong?

The 1960s were haunted by images of desolation as well as hope. Eleanor Rigby, in the song by Lennon and McCartney, had no one to love her or even notice her existence. Her life slipped by, anonymous. Her funeral was unattended, except by the ineffectual priest, 'No one was saved.' The vision remains as powerful as ever across three decades, 'all the lonely people' flowing past us 'where do they all come from?'

At the same time as The Beatles were singing their elegy to loneliness, John Hopkins was writing a television quartet called 'Talking to a Stranger'. His heroine, Terry, is facing life as a single parent, anguished and alone. She cries out:

> 'Why is it so lonely . . . I want to live in a crowd of ten thousand – and never let one of them go home. I want them

round me, all round me – day and night – loving me.'

Now the talk of community has come full circle again, after the materialism and isolation of the last twenty years. At the beginning of the decade, there were fine sentiments about the 'caring nineties', but the Terries and Eleanor Rigbys are still with us. Perhaps we are like them.

In fact, the more our society goes on about 'community', the more some people feel left out – and this includes the 'up-and-out' as well as the 'down-and-out'. Stress isolates. It traps us in pain. We are under pressure and carrying the load by ourselves. We desperately need support, to be 'upheld'.

To be 'upheld' is a telling physical image but it is a rare experience for many. The only 'togetherness' they experience is the meaningless crush of a tube train, and the only community the sad isolation of city bars where people shout their orders over the din of strange voices. Some people look for support in groups but don't find it. They join bogus communities, like clubs where no one really meets or identifies with another, or even churches, where the spaces between people say more than the sermons. The old arrive and depart alone. The needy go on their way, unloved. 'No one is saved.'

To discover real togetherness is to alleviate stress. A moment of shared experience can make a profound difference to the way we feel about life. Such liberating experiences may have nothing to do with pouring out our problems but with joy – the thrill of a sports crowd, the throng of a pop festival at 3 a.m., joining a hundred thousand people to get dripping wet with Pavarotti in Hyde Park. There are times when it isn't lonely to be in a crowd. It all depends which crowd.

Terry, in 'Talking to a Stranger', dreams of a crowd 'all round me – day and night – loving me' because her own family has failed her. Sometimes, at the heart of our stress, there is a painfully deep, family-shaped hole.

Families

The hole in our lives may be there because our childhood home was 'dysfunctional', broken, troubled. Or the hole may be there because we have left our finest support system – a loving family – hundreds of miles away, to go to college or work or because we are 'upwardly mobile' (and inwardly on our own).

An advert in a magazine once read:

'Choose your parents carefully.'

It's revealing, if unhelpful, advice. We may have some other choices though. One is to put living in the context of an extended family higher on the agenda than money. The increasing fragmentation of the old network of support, grandparents, uncles, aunts, parents, family friends, is a sad but not necessarily unalterable fact of modern life. Personally, we may be able to change that by adjusting our priorities. A couple, likely to have children, should consider carefully whether to do so in an isolated situation, whatever the financial rewards.

An extended family is often the best kind of support a person can ever get. Many do not have such families or such opportunities. Those who do, especially those with children, need to look carefully at how they are replacing this 'infra-structure' of love if they move away.

However, it is painfully obvious that the wider family can be a source of severe stress too. Those who support practically may also interfere and undermine. Family relationships that are too close and possessive may hurt as well as heal. The psychotherapist Robin Skynner, who co-authored the book *Families and How to Survive Them* with John Cleese, summed up problem families as those which are 'too close or too far apart'. Claustrophobic intensity or uncaring remoteness are obviously counter-productive extremes.

It is important to attempt some kind of objective view of the extended family network and how it operates, if we are to make the best of its support. The most constructive back-up gives a person a sense of relief in sharing problems with another: but also of independence in making up his or her mind about what action to take. Close relatives can provide this in the healthiest families. Yet it is worth remembering that the worst sort of support is when a relative – or friend – colludes with a person in a false diagnosis of the problem. 'You should get out of your marriage' can be damaging advice, when marital problems are not so much the cause but the symptom of deeper stresses, which may even have their roots a long way back in childhood.

Advice can be very influential when it comes from a highly valued source like a parent. Yet the dangers of giving advice which is too strong – and wrong – need to be recognised. A father is not likely to say to his son 'Take my views with a pinch of salt', nor a mother to say 'Ring me less often to ask my opinion', so choosing close relatives as our main source of support requires careful evaluation of the advice given. However close and loving our extended family is, we need to maintain our independence psychologically.

Dual-career partnerships

The slogan 'MAKE LOVE NOT WAR' was painted on a wall – and underneath a graffiti artist had added 'I'm married. I do both'.

It goes without saying that the immediate family context is often the greatest source of conflict, as well as of comfort, in our lives. In the delicate balance of human emotions which make up a love relationship, an extra weight – like financial pressures or illness – can easily upset our equilibrium.

Perhaps the most difficult of all partnerships, although potentially very rewarding, is the dual-career relationship. It is increasingly common for both partners to work in full-time employment, as well as run a home and attempt to bring up children too. A battle for survival is then being waged on three fronts – and stretched-out battlelines often end in defeat. It is a familiar cause of anguish to many women that they are bearing the brunt of domestic responsibilities whilst trying to earn a living. The 'New Man' has not, in reality, come of age – and the cooking, child-rearing, domesticated male, one who would if necessary put his partner's career before his own, is still the exception that proves the rule. Some husbands and boyfriends are more accurately described as 'Ambivalent New Men': wanting to help in the home, to take a full part in the children's upbringing, but secretly resentful of their wife's or girlfriend's unavailability. Deep down, perhaps too deep to admit, they still feel that home life is *her* responsibility. This ambivalence is stressful in itself – the attempt to fulfil a new role against a background of prejudice and preconceptions, often arising from parental pressures, or even the comments of older female relatives and friends: 'Can't she work part-time?', 'You shouldn't have to be doing all this.' No one, however, seems to be saying this to the woman who feels that she is enslaved by household chores. Such tensions often produce a no-win situation in which both partners lose out on the love and support that they need to pursue their careers and, needless to say, the children are affected more by tensions in the home than by whether their parents go out to work or not.

Sympathetic insight is needed on both sides. The woman who joked about being married to a model husband (see 'Romanticism', p. 86) is making a fair point – but perhaps it is also fair to recognise that idealistic expectations can wreak havoc in our relationships. No one is perfect – there is simply the reality of a given relationship and learning how, given the facts about two jobs, to negotiate roles fairly. This may mean simple devices like preparing balance sheets of work and home commitments, and maybe calling family meetings to discuss different jobs and the areas of communal living that are under threat: 'Is there any way you can give me more time on a Saturday morning? I feel I'm left alone with the children'; 'Why don't we agree to discuss all social commitments first, before packing our diaries and leaving no time to be together?' Children can be encouraged, as well, to play a more responsible role – they need incentives, rewards as well as appreciation. They need to know where they fit in and that their contribution is important. It is easy to forget that school children are going out to work too and facing considerable stresses as they grow up. Whole families need to present a united front to a difficult and demanding world.

However, despite our best efforts, the conflicts of interest in dual-career relationships can sometimes reach crisis point. When they do, it is essential to find ways of lowering the temperature. Bebe Campbell-Moore, in her book *Successful Women, Angry Men*, suggests these steps:

1 Find time to talk in a relaxed way. This may involve deliberately setting aside some time from busy schedules when lack of interruptions is guaranteed.

2 Learn techniques of effective communication. Using the wrong words can alienate. It is better to take responsibility for your own feelings and behaviour than to accuse. For example, to say 'I feel you could do more in the house' rather than 'You never do enough in the house'. Your feelings can be discussed, but an accusation merely makes the other person defensive.

3 Listen to what the other person says. It is useful to reflect back, to show that you have really heard and accept his or her feelings. For example, 'It sounds as though you feel really angry with me. Can you tell me what it is that I do which makes you feel that way?'

If problems have become really overwhelming:

4 It might help to agree an official time out or call a temporary truce. A temporary separation, such as separate holidays, may provide time to work out a solution.

5 Don't try to solve all problems at once. Work on one at a time.

6 If necessary, elicit the help of a professional counsellor.

Friends

Friends, neighbours, colleagues and other support groups which are beyond our personal 'circle of stress' are an important part of keeping our balance in times of crisis.

Friendship is an art to be cultivated. Unlike blood relatives, we choose our friends. It is vital to choose well. Too many men, in particular, are friendless. They have acquaintances, colleagues they drink with, a golfing partner perhaps, or they like to be 'one of the lads'. They will sit and drink for hours but never really talk or share themselves. Most men fear vulnerability – which makes them far more vulnerable in a crisis. Women, frequently more honest about themselves and their worries, often have a wider circle of friends and at least one person they can have a 'heart-to-heart' with. It is sad how out of touch a lot of men are with their feelings, often because they do not open their hearts to anyone. They have never done it with friends, so even a partner or wife can be excluded. Good, trusting friendship is one of the keys to survival.

However, friends can add to our stresses too, if they are not sufficiently detached. The ideal friend is someone who can stand back from our problems when we can't, share, sympathise, weep with us, restore our sense of humour and perspective – but a wise friend may also gently challenge us to rethink our position too. One of the pictures in the Bayeux Tapestry shows King Harold prodding his soldiers' backsides with a spear. An early translation of the inscription reads: 'King Harold comforts his soldiers'.

To comfort someone, in the earliest sense of the word, is to encourage, to help us move on. Sympathy is vital in bereavement at all stages, and we need our friends to identify with our darkest feelings over a long period of time. But we need their resources too, their hope, their courage. Their belief in us that we can develop, move on. We need a prod or two to help us out of the past, into the present. We need 'comforting' into a new stage of our lives.

This combination of sympathetic understanding and encouragement is the hallmark of the most precious friendships. Learning to recognise this quality can help to determine the kind of friend to avoid in a crisis.

First of all, there are those who avoid us when we are in trouble, the well-known 'Fairweather Friends', but such people are not worthy of the title 'friend'. More complex are those who do care, but care in an unhelpful way, or add their own problems on to ours. Take, for example, the 'Worrier-on-your-behalf'. This is the kind of friend who doesn't let you finish a sentence because they've thought of three more worrying aspects of your problem already. 'Oh dear, how are you going to manage that?', 'But you can't possibly cope with all this', 'What on earth are you going to do?' It's hard to distinguish this from genuine sympathetic concern, but it is important to ask yourself whether the Worrier's attitude is constructive. Does it make you feel better talking to this person? That simple question is the touchstone for discerning a true friend. Many people who have suffered greatly find that they have been coping quite well, on a particular day, until they meet an old friend whose pained sympathy on their behalf actually weakens their ability to cope. In such cases:

- Don't let the Worrier-on-your-behalf distort *your* perspective.
- Tell yourself 'Perhaps they couldn't cope, but I can'.
- Seek out another friend who affirms your ability to cope.

Apart from the Worrier, there are a few other types of friend to avoid in a crisis:

- ***The Job's Comforter***. (Adds guilt: 'You've really brought this one on yourself.')
- ***The Expert***. (Blind to the uniqueness of your personality: 'I've been through all this before.' He hasn't.)
- ***The Critic***. (Never at a loss for more people to blame: 'I wouldn't trust the new area manager either, if I were you – he's a swine.' Delights in adding fuel to the fire.)
- ***The Personal Organiser***. (Takes over your life: 'This is what you must do and how you must do it and the order in which you must do it.' Demoralises you with plans for your life which are usually wrong.)

Stress could be reduced in our lives if we turned to the right kind of friends. Often, even in a limited social circle, there is at least one person who is discreet and reliable. It may be a colleague at work, whose integrity is apparent, or a neighbour whose warmth and gentle manner mark them out. There is nothing manipulative about 'cultivating friendship'.

It may well be that the closest friends are the oldest ones – but we have lost touch, perhaps because of the hectic pace and social mobility of our lives. We should consider renewing contact because, in finding old friends again, we may find ourselves.

Yet it is true that some people, particularly Type As, have difficulty establishing healthy relationships that depend on trust. Rather than making new friends, they collect enemies. Their barely hidden hostility – a general attitude to the world – spills over into their workplace and their social lives. Friedman and Rosenmann offer more advice to the Type As who need to learn how their behaviour affects others:

1. Try to make yourself aware of the impact your behaviour has on other people. 'If you are overly hostile, certainly one of the most important drill measures you should adopt is that one in which you remind yourself of the fact that you are hostile.'
2. Try to value the efforts of other people and reward them. 'Begin to speak your thanks or appreciation to others when they have performed services for you. And do not do so, like so many hostile Type A subjects, with merely a grunt of thanks.' Such responses may seem a little forced to begin with, but they can help to start a new process – a different way of behaving which will eventually override the old aggressive pattern. Try affirming people more, talking to them in a relaxed and positive way, greeting them regularly. Take an interest in their lives outside the workplace. Set time aside to develop social relationships.
3. Type As often blame other people for not meeting their ideals, or pick on the shortcomings of their colleagues as

> the reason for their own failures or disappointments. 'Over and over again, we have listened to Type As rationalise their hostility as stemming from disappointment over the lack of ideals in their friends. We always have advised such sick people that they should cease trying to be "idealists" because they are in fact only looking for excuses to be disappointed and hence hostile towards others.'

Friendship is a two-way matter, a 'mutual comfort society'. Friendship needs to be earned. Trust has to be established and even if we become dependent on our friends at times, they must also be able to depend on us when they are in trouble. The self-obsessed person ultimately has few friends.

Community

Our relationship with the wider community we live in is also a significant factor in our support system. Clubs, societies, adult education, charities, sports centres, all help to widen our circle. 'No man is an island' wrote the poet John Donne – but many of us behave as if we are. Our island may be literal isolation from others, but it may also be keeping to a very limited circle of like-minded peers. This means restricting our lives to others who suffer from similar stresses and who may increase ours. If we only ever mix with colleagues from work, we never escape from the pressures. If we only see our families, domestic issues dominate. Broadening our lives is crucial to perspective on our own stresses. The young need the old. The old gain strength from the young.

It may be extremely difficult to cross some barriers, not least the barriers of class and culture which are still so unyielding in many parts of Britain – but community activity that brings together different backgrounds as well as different age groups can be liberating. When we are under stress we can benefit profoundly from variety of experience, from an insight into other lives which can help us to step outside the air-tight compartments and 'ghettos' which we have often inherited.

Self-help groups

It has to be admitted, though, that sometimes we are so crippled by a particular problem – it might be alcoholism or depression – that we simply cannot go out into the community and make new friends. In such cases, we may first need to be with others who are fellow sufferers. Self-help groups are another way of bringing our problems into a situation of community. We are not alone.

Alcoholics Anonymous, Weight Watchers, Depressives Anonymous, smoking and tranquilliser addiction groups, self-help for phobics and those who suffer from panic attacks – there is a wide variety of such groups.

It is worth singling out one recent development, which is 'Co-dependency' groups. Co-dependants are people who are described as suffering from 'addictive relationships'. Often from a background of alcoholism or chemical dependency in their family, or where there has been a great pressure to keep up appearances, co-dependants often feel the need to please, to care endlessly for others. They suffer from overwhelming feelings of guilt and rage, negative emotions towards those they are caring for, because frequently their own childhood has forced them into a relationship of caring for 'problem parents'. There are useful books on co-dependency and a number of self-help groups have arisen to help these sufferers, who often appear to be 'coping well' but are dangerously vulnerable to depressive illness and relationship problems.

Counselling and medical support

Ultimately, we may need to admit that our problems have gone too far for families, friends and self-help groups to provide adequate support. When they cannot help us to survive and recover, we must go further.

Some people think of all professional counselling as a dangerous indulgence. They have visions of decadent Californians enjoying a perpetual ego-massage from their therapists, who enrich themselves at the expense of their gullible clientele. There may be a grain of truth here in some cases. But the caricature image is also a helpful shield to hide behind. There are plenty of people who would prefer not to be helped. If we know, and we often do, that we are in the grip of a serious problem, whether behavioural (addiction) or psychological (depression, obsession) we must take medical advice.

It is important to discover the attitude of your GP to psychiatric help. Some doctors are knowledgeable and sympathetic, others have very little experience of this area. Pills are sometimes dispensed by busy GPs who do not have the time or training to discern cases which need psychiatric referral – which often comes far too late. To be fair to the average doctor, he or she is often presented with a bewildering array of psychosomatic complaints every week and it is all too easy to miss the warning signs of a serious clinical depression. Easy but disastrous for patients and their families – and if medical negligence cases were extended to wrong diagnosis in psychological as well as physiological cases, such oversights could prove professionally disastrous to many doctors.

There is an urgent need to broaden medical training here. However, accepting the 'pot-luck' element in the present system, it may be necessary to look for a doctor who can demonstrate understanding and give informed advice on the options available. If there is no one like this in a particular practice, there is no alternative but to be extremely persistent on your own behalf – or, more likely, on behalf of a relative – if you have decided that psychiatric or psychotherapeutic help is the next important step and you need to seek assistance through the National Health Service. It is possible to find a variety of counselling services through the NHS, including behavioural psychology, psychotherapy and psycho-sexual counselling, and it is worth pursuing this course as far as you can.

Dr Robin Skynner described the purpose of psychotherapy in an article in the *Weekend Guardian*, 21 September 1991:

'Good psychotherapy helps people to help themselves. It is

quite unlike major surgery, where you don't participate at all but remain passive, indeed unconscious, while someone does something to you. It is more a joint exploration, where the therapist is like a guide with a general knowledge of an area and of map-reading, who is trying to help you find your lost home from details you remember. Only you will recognise it when you find it.'

Although seeking help at this level is a recognition of a deep need, it is also a courageous decision which requires commitment. It is not a sign of weakness to seek help from psychotherapists or psychiatrists. It is a sign of strength. It means facing up to pain and vulnerability and looking for a way through, however slowly or uncertainly. The weak people are those who refuse help and continue to deny the seriousness of their problems.

> 'There is no special rule about when it is right to go for counselling, but I guess I'd say it's when you find yourself increasingly unable to cope with your own feelings and there is nobody amongst your friends and relatives and colleagues whom you can talk to, probably because your friends, relatives and colleagues are part of the problem. So to get somebody who is right outside of that situation and who will be prepared just to sit and listen to you for a certain amount of time and perhaps offer some wise comments, that's what you need. Don't just let that situation go on and on, where you feel worse and worse and more and more trapped and more and more alone.'

(Dorothy Rowe, psychologist, from the TV series, *Relax*, BBC/ Prospect Pictures, 1992)

Lindsay Knight's book *Talking to a Stranger* is recommended by Robin Skynner as a guide to the various types of therapy and the centres which provide them.

One kind of therapy which has become available in recent years is called cognitive therapy. This helps patients to solve their own problems by learning to see things differently and by discovering hidden resources of strength. In some ways, it is a development of the well-worn strategy of 'positive thinking', but not in any glib or shallow way. If anxiety, for example, cannot be eliminated, then it can be managed instead. Sufferers from panic attacks can find this approach very helpful. One former Valium addict, who found release from her problems through a cognitive therapy course at the Warneford Hospital, Oxford, explained:

> 'I've had to accept I'm a worrier. It's never going to go away. My mother was the same and so is my brother. But what I have to be very careful about is that it doesn't spread. That's why it is very important to identify your thoughts – to make sure hundreds of other things don't pile in.'
>
> (From an article in the *Evening Standard*, 29 July 1991)

There are courses at the Maudsley Hospital in London, too, and cognitive therapy is gradually becoming more available elsewhere.

In the biblical parable of the Prodigal Son, the young man leaves home and recklessly spends his inheritance on 'riotous living'. He lands up in a country hit by economic recession, penniless and facing starvation. He takes the lowliest job of all, feeding the pigs. In a modern version of the story, no doubt he would adopt a typical Type A solution to his problem: 'I'll take over the pigsty – get into the pigswill business – establish a chain of agricultural supply stores – claw my way back to a fortune!' However, in the original story, the young man decides to go back to the source of his low self-esteem – his failed relationship with his father.

Profound 'positive thinking' may mean accepting that we cannot cope without going back to basics, and sorting out a fundamental relationship problem with the help of counsellors.

Reality checkpoints

Having said all this about the enormous value of good counselling, it is worth stepping back for a moment and reflecting on the choices before us. A wise perspective on our own lives is always essentially hopeful. It includes a belief in our potential for change, and shuns passivity or cynicism. But it will also include a healthy degree of scepticism. It is one thing to recognise an urgent need; another to accept a particular solution to our problems because it is fashionable or because someone else has told us what to do.

Our century began with the invention (Freud would have said 'scientific discovery') of psychoanalysis, and has ended with what some would call 'the culture of therapy'. It is shrewd, especially for those who choose therapy or long-term counselling, to reserve their own judgement about the process and to be aware of dangers. Perhaps the main one is handing over to a therapist or a counsellor a degree of influence which we would never give to anyone else and entering a world without checks or balances. The influence of the therapist, if the process becomes too all pervasive, is extremely subtle. It is certainly not like the obvious negative influence of a domineering parent, or an autocratic boss, or a dogmatic priest. It appears to be the very opposite of such 'emotional oppression' – but it may not be. In the guise of silence, listening, gentle questioning, suspending all judgement and blame, reassuring smiles and a self-effacing role which reveals nothing of his own personal life, the therapist can become extremely powerful. Terms like 'transference' and 'countertransference' can disguise what is truly happening. Ever since Freud wrote his monumental work, *The Interpretation of Dreams* – describing dreams as the 'royal road to the Unconscious' – there has been a danger of the therapist holding some kind of golden key to the inner, lost world of the psyche. Patients or 'clients' can believe fervently that they are unlocking their own dreams and coming to understand so much more about their unconscious motivation. In fact, they may be absorbing the world view of the therapist, and of therapy in particular, which can often insidiously affect everything including family relationships, marriage, career, religious belief. It is healthy to be aware of such dangers, and the best and the most conscientious therapists are aware of them too.

A friend of one of the authors, wandering through the fog across some parkland in Cambridge, came across a lamppost – which loomed out of the grey expanse. On the lamppost, standing alone in this sea of fog, someone had scrawled: 'reality checkpoint'. It is vital to have 'reality checkpoints' if we are undergoing any kind of serious counselling, even though the counselling itself may well seem the greatest reality of all in the midst of trouble. This may be so – the honesty of a therapeutic situation can be a great relief after years of pretending or hiding from our wounds – but it may not be so. If counselling or therapy has a sound basis to it, the process will gain from other perspectives too – a variety of 'reality checkpoints' in a world of emotional confusion. The best strategy is to add the insights of friendships, other forms of advice, personnel at work, pastoral advice in colleges or churches or within self-help groups, sympathetic relatives or colleagues who are not too closely involved and can offer a 'sounding board' at critical moments. As individuals we need to live in a psychological democracy, in which we still have the vote, and in which dissenting voices – including our own – can still be heard. We must never hand ourselves over, accidentally, to a miniature totalitarian regime run by a counsellor – or, for that matter, by any kind of secular or religious 'guru' (see the section on p. 85 on 'fanaticism'). This kind of 'psychological addiction' to a person or a group is a short route to multiplying our problems.

But there are issues beyond the question of whether therapy or counselling is the right option for any of us facing serious crisis. The wider issues raised are often to do with how we choose to see the world, and whether we can be enabled to look beyond our own individual self at all. Midway through the book, we spoke of hope and the need to find a view past our own ego. The wrong kind of therapy, although intended to renew hope, can sometimes block that essential view. A short story, written for a workshop on stress, can illustrate the problem more vividly:

'There was once a beautiful butterfly who had a broken wing. He tried to fly but he moved round in circles. He bumped into trees and went fluttering to the ground. He felt as though his life had come to an end. The butterfly was very beautiful, with deep yellow and blue patterns, bright streaks of colour, long sensitive antennae – but he could not fly. He could not be what he was meant to be.

He went to the butterfly doctors, but they couldn't help him. He went to his butterfly friends but they became tired of his complaints and his sadness. He tried butterfly counsellors of many kinds but their advice was all contradictory – some said "go to sleep", some said "exercise", some gave him herbal medicine.

But still he couldn't fly.

At last he found an alternative butterfly therapist who was very kind and loving and listened to him a great deal. She told him that his despair was quite understandable because everyone had failed him. She told him not to blame himself. She told him that his self was what really mattered, that he needed to express himself, that he needed to find the inner butterfly within; that, if necessary, he should question all his existing relationships. No one understood better than she did what he needed, which was to express his rage and find himself, to find the butterfly god within his soul.

He went to her for many, many sessions, and her words comforted him, and as she listened and as she spoke, he found he was spinning a soft gossamer all around himself. He was rebuilding his chrysalis. Now he knew he would find himself, because his own self was all that mattered. There was nothing beyond and certainly nothing more important than this.

At last he was enclosed in a huge chrysalis. He was wrapped up in himself completely. His wing was still broken, it was still painful, and now there was no chance of him flying at all. But none of these things seemed to matter much any more. His desire, which had once been very simple, was to be healed. But slowly, imperceptibly, he had lost all hope of that.

> Anyway, he didn't need that. After all, in his dark, impenetrable chrysalis, he had found himself – and wasn't that all that really mattered?'
>
> (Watts, stress seminar, London, 1994)

New perspectives

It is always tempting, in times of crisis, to opt out from giving to others. We are deeply conscious of our own needs. We must get ourselves 'sorted out' first. In the very worst situations, we can be like a drowning person who drags down his rescuers in the struggle to survive. But, paradoxically, our own survival may depend on our readiness to reach out to others.

There is something of this in the philosophy behind Anita Roddick's programme with employees of the Body Shop, which was launched a few years ago. Once a month, thirty members of staff were seconded to community projects in areas of need, as far as Romania, for a period of two or three weeks. Rather than send her people on outward bound courses, which concentrate on personal fitness and physical renewal, she focused on service. By becoming bonded with different age groups, needs and even cultures, by doing some good for others, individual morale and purpose can be dramatically improved at the same time as enriching others.

For most of us, the only opportunities lie in the local community. There are no enlightened employers to pay for such experiences. We must be enlightened ourselves – and, where possible, make the lives and needs of others our business. Dealing with our own problems can be like 'Alice Through the Looking Glass' – in order to reach a place, we may have to walk away from it. This does not mean 'escaping' from our problems but walking away from our own self-obsession and into the needs of others.

According to the sociologist Abraham Maslow, service is the highest form of human need. Survival is our most basic requirement, but that is often where we get stuck, fighting our own battles. The need for security comes next, then belonging, then achievement, but service is the ultimate need. This is the final freedom.

Service may well seem impossible to the stressed person and the idea of helping anyone else – 'When I've got so much on my plate!' – can be met with scorn. But learning to consider the needs of others seriously is to evolve to a more advanced form of life.

Evolution is exactly what is needed in dealing with stress. We must change. A heightened sense of purpose, as we have seen earlier in the book, can give meaning to our pain. It may not cure it, make all our stresses go away, but a sense of the value of what we do can help us to cope. Serving, not just a cause or an ideal, but people, can help us find our own identity. The quality of our relationships, at home or at work, whether employed or unemployed, is a much more important gauge of our achievements than traditional ideas of 'success' or 'failure'. The build up of stress, which can so easily destroy, can provide a vantage point from which we can gain a vital new perspective on the rest of our life.

There are many steps we can take – sometimes simple and sometimes difficult and demanding – when we are determined to reduce the impact of stress on our lives. However, nothing is more difficult than living with a severely stressed person and feeling powerless to help them. Their crisis can easily affect us for the worse even as we try to 'pull them through'. Learning to live with a stressed person is really a book in itself, but the following advice may be helpful.

Living with a stressed person

- People under severe stress lose their perspective. Try to keep yours.
- Don't let their stress infect you, making you anxious. The problems will get much worse if you add to them. Use mental and physical relaxation exercises. Find space and time to be alone.

- Don't get drawn into endless rows. Your anger will serve to justify the anger of the other person, which needs exposing as a problem.
- Be kind to yourself. Don't be a martyr. The carer needs caring for too. Make sure you have at least one person you can off-load your problems on to. Express your anger and frustrations to them. Clear the air regularly.
- Look for 'early warning' signs of stress in those you love. Choose a moment when your partner or relative is calm and relaxed. Gently point out your concern to them, without any accusation. 'I'm worried about you. You're smoking a lot more than you used to. You must feel under a lot of strain.'
- Take action on their behalf in cases where their will is paralysed. 'I think we should talk about your depression to our doctor. Let me make an appointment. I'll come with you.'
- When resistance to any change is put up, over a long period, be firm. You cannot go on listening to the same gripes and moans thousands of times without your relationship deteriorating. Be loving but make it clear that you are not only a son, daughter, wife, but a person in your own right with your own needs. You need them to find a way through.
- Be a 'sounding-board' but not a 'duck-board'. If your feelings are being ignored and you are being trodden down, insist on some time away, a day, a weekend, with friends or alone. Keep renewing your strength.
- Don't be a 'co-dependant', worsening the stressed person's problems by your need to care for them. Don't hold back their progress by indulging them – because it makes you feel 'needed'. Their self-destructive attitudes or behaviour can never be the foundation for a healthy relationship.
- Be an 'enabler'. See yourself as the one who helps the sufferer to help themselves.
- Help them to focus on the present and the future. To talk about what can be done, not what cannot be undone.
- Try making a list of problem areas in their life. Do it together. Look at some options.

- Believe for them that things can change, without being unsympathetic or glib. Be their eyes when they can't see beyond their problems. Remind them that this is temporary. They will see clearly and hope again.

Epilogue: Choosing to Live

'The most dangerous thing in the world is living. There's a 100 per cent mortality rate.'

Birth and death are two experiences which all human beings share, but there's a third which affects the quality of all that happens in between: stress. How we handle stress affects our whole life. It may even affect the length of our life. A journalist arrived at the funeral of a high-flying executive who had dropped dead at the age of forty-five. 'How much did he leave?' whispered the journalist to a mourner. 'Everything,' came the reply.

The simplest question which we often ask when under the greatest duress is 'What's the point of it all?' and yet, somehow, we don't stop long enough to find an answer. We are always running out of time, hurrying, chasing. 'Sorry, I haven't got time.' But we have. Plenty of time – but we have to take it away from the things that don't matter.

Changing our priorities is one of the themes of this book. Another, and by far the most important, is that we must take responsibility for our own life and wellbeing. Ultimately, we must give up blaming external circumstances or other people for the difficulty of our lives, however tempting it may be, and however many proofs we can offer to ourselves and to others that the problems are 'out there'. This is a point made emphatically by leading writers on stress. It was also made by the playwright George Bernard Shaw in his play *Mrs Warren's Profession*.

> 'People are always blaming their circumstances for what they are. I don't believe in circumstances. The people who get on

> in this world are the people who get up and look for the circumstances they want, and if they can't find them, make them.'

A person who sees himself or herself as the helpless victim of stress can become so uptight that finally everything becomes a crisis, an overwhelming effort. Life appears impossible, but this is an illusion. There are things we can do. We can take the principle of 'tough love' to heart. We must love ourselves and that means believing in ourselves – and taking on the challenge of our own lives.

Failure to adapt successfully to change is at the root of stress. More often than not, we cannot prevent stressful changes in our circumstances or our lives. But our aim should be to stop the wrong kind of change in ourselves which comes as a reaction to events. The slide into bitterness or self-destructive behaviour is slow but deadly. Stress can kill emotionally as well as physically and, in many ways, that is a worse kind of death to suffer. It can also be a 'bereavement' which is agonising for those living with the stressed person. 'What happened to the person I married?' can be a fair and searching question. Rather than others pointing out such disastrous changes, we need to anticipate them. The question we must ask ourselves is, 'What kind of changes am I going to encourage in myself?'

Stress is infectious, but so is love. Finding a way through for ourselves will almost certainly enrich the lives of others.

Back to the beginning

Perhaps the most fundamental change of all is to go back to the beginning. To start again with new insight. To see a simple truth from a shattering new perspective.

> We shall not cease from exploration
> And the end of all our exploring
> Will be to arrive where we started
> And know the place for the first time.

(T S Eliot, *Four Quartets*)

In the moving film *Awakenings*, based on the true story by Dr Oliver Sacks, a doctor liberates his patients from a terrible mental and physical wilderness by experimenting with a new drug. Lost for decades in a trance-like state of inactivity, the sufferers from this rare condition suddenly experience life as if for the first time.

Leonard, played by Robert de Niro, calls the doctor up in the middle of the night with an urgent message. The doctor hurries round to the hospital. Leonard, who has lost all the best years of his life, is overflowing with energy and excitement: 'We've got to tell everybody. We've got to remind them how good it is!' Dr Sayer, played by Robin Williams, is bewildered. But Leonard is unstoppable. He seizes a newspaper:

> 'Read the newspaper. What does it say? All bad. It's all bad. People have forgotten what life is all about. They've forgotten what it is to be alive. They need to be reminded – they need to be reminded about what they have and what they can lose.' Leonard, in his brief period of living again, gives his testimony to the world: 'What I feel is the joy of life, the gift of life, the freedom of life, the wonderment of life!'
>
> (Screenplay by Steven Zaillian from the Penny Marshall film *Awakenings*, Columbia Pictures)

Far from wanting the world to stop, Leonard is keen to get on and ride with it, to make exciting new discoveries and to reclaim all the potential of his life.

The freed hostage John McCarthy described the joy of looking out of a window and seeing daylight, after four years' captivity in the dark. He had recovered the simple pleasure of being alive. He had survived.

And we can too. One day at a time, maybe one painful step at a time, we can find our way out of the prison of stress and learn how to live again. Then we can discover what perhaps we knew so long ago as children – how to love life.

Books to Read

There are many books on stress, ranging across a wide variety of subjects. Health and 'self-help' sections in bookshops and libraries are worth exploring, but the following recommendations can be a preliminary guide.

GENERAL BOOKS ON STRESS

Stress Relief
Sharon Faelten and David Diamond London: Ebury Press 1989
Living with Stress
Cary L Cooper, Rachel D Cooper and Lynne H Eaker London: Penguin Books 1988
Managing Workplace Stress
Sue Cartwright and Cary L Cooper London: Sage 1997

STRESS AND RELAXATION

The Complete Guide to Stress Management
Chandra Patel London: Optima 1989
Stress and Relaxation
Jane Madders London: Optima 1988

STRESS AND WORK

Coping with Stress at Work
Jacqueline M Atkinson London: Thorsons 1988
Handbook of Coping
Moshe Zeidner and Norman Endler New York: Wiley and Sons 1996

TYPE A BEHAVIOUR

Type A Behaviour and Your Heart
M D Friedman and R H Rosenmann New York: Knopf 1974
Living in Overdrive
Clive Wood London: Fontana 1984

BIOFEEDBACK TRAINING

Stress and the Art of Biofeedback
Barbara Brown London: Bantam 1978

STRESS AND WOMEN

Coping with Stress: A Woman's Guide
Dr Georgia Witkin-Lanoil London: Sheldon Press 1985
Successful Women: Angry Men
Bebe Campbell-Moore London: Arrow 1988
A Woman in Your Own Right
Anne Dickson London: Quartet Books 1982
Managing Your Career and Family: Getting the Balance Right
Cary L Cooper and Sue Lewis London: Kogan Page

ASSERTIVENESS TRAINING

Assertiveness: The Right to Be You
Claire Walmsley (accompanying the BBC Series *Tomorrow – The World*) London: BBC Books 1991
Improving Interpersonal Relations
Edited by Cary L Cooper with a section on Assertiveness Training by Sandra Langrish Epping: Gowen Press 1981
(*See also*: **A Woman in Your Own Right** above)

DUAL-CAREER COUPLES

Career Couples: Contemporary Lifestyles and How to Manage Them
Suzan Lewis and Cary L Cooper London: Unwin 1989
The Workplace Revolution: Managing Today's Dual Career Families
London: Kogan Page 1993

FAMILIES

Families and How to Survive Them

Robin Skynner and John Cleese London: Methuen 1984

PSYCHOTHERAPY

Talking to a Stranger

Lindsay Knight London: Fontana 1986

DEPRESSION

Overcoming Depression: The Way Out of Your Prison

Dorothy Rowe London: Routledge and Kegan Paul 1989

The Independent Health Guide to Depression and How it can be Treated

Jeremy Laurance A booklet available from the *Independent* newspaper, London

Darkness Visible

William Styron London: Jonathan Cape 1991

CO-DEPENDENCY

Codependency: How to Break Free and Live Your Own Life

David Stafford and Liz Hodginson London: Piatkus 1991

ME

Why M. E.? A Guide to Combating Post-Viral Illness

Dr Belinda Dawes and Dr Damien Downing London: Grafton Books 1989

BEREAVEMENT

Through Grief: The Bereavement Journey

Published in association with CRUSE (*see* Useful Addresses)

DIET AND HEALTH

The BBC Diet

Dr Barry Lynch London: BBC Books 1989

Don't Break Your Heart

Dr Barry Lynch London: Sidgwick and Jackson 1987

OTHER BOOKS AND ARTICLES REFERRED TO

Stress and the Manager: Making it Work for You
Karl Albrecht New Jersey: Prentice-Hall 1979

'Psychological Stress and Coping Process'
Richard Lazarus New York: McGraw-Hill 1966

'A Short Rating Scale as a Potential Measure of Type A Behaviour'
R W Bortner *Journal of Chronic Diseases* 22 (1969) 87–91

'Stressful Life Events. Personality, Health: an Enquiry into Hardiness'
Suzanne Kobasa *Journal of Personality and Social Psychology*, vol. 37 (1939)

The Person: Development Through the Life Cycle
T Lidz New York: Basic Books 1968

Your Erroneous Zones
Wayne Dyer New York: Avon Books 1976

Structural Experiences for Human Relations Training
Bill Pfeiffer and John Jones Iowa City: University Associates Press 1970

Organizational Stress and Preventive Management
J C Quick and J D Quick New York: McGraw-Hill 1984

Stress in Teaching
Jack Dunham London: Croom Helm 1984

Handbook of Work and Health Psychology
A Schabracq, J Winnubst and C Chichester John Wiley and Sons 1996

Handbook of Stress, Medicine and Health
C Cooper Florida: CRC Press 1996

'Generalized Expectations for Internal vs External Control of Reinforcement'
J B Rotter *Psychology Monograph* 80 (1966)

Stress and Disease
H G Wolff Illinois: Charles and Thomas 1953

Useful Addresses

(Remember to send a stamped addressed envelope when writing in for information)

Alcoholics Anonymous
PO Box 1
Stonebow House
Stonebow
York YO1 2NJ
01904 644026/7/8/9
(24-hr telephone service
0171-352 3001)

Action on Smoking and Health (ASH)
16 Fitzharding Street
London W1H 9PL
Information and lists of local authority smoking clinics

Alcohol Concern
Waterbridge House
32–6 Loman Street
London SE1 0EE
0171-928 7377
Information and referrals for counselling

Age Concern (England)
Astral House
1268 London Road
London SW16 4ER
0181-679 8000

The Chemical Dependency Centre
11 Redcliffe Gardens
London SW10 9BG
0171-352 2552

Codependents Anonymous
PO Box 1292
London N4 2YX
CODA is for anyone who recognises a problem of co-dependency and is seeking help

St Joseph's Centre for Addiction
Holy Cross Hospital
Hindhead Road
Haslemere

Surrey GU27 1NQ
01428 656517

As well as dealing with drug and alcohol dependency, St Joseph's has a co-dependency clinic

Cruse
Cruse House
126 Sheen Road
Richmond
Surrey TW9 1UR
0181-940 4818
Help for those suffering from bereavement

Depressives Anonymous
36 Chestnut Avenue
Beverley
East Yorkshire HU17 9QU
01482 860619
A self-help organisation for people with depression

MIND
Granta House
15–19 Broadway
Stratford
London E15 4BQ
0181-519 2122
Information on all aspects of mental health

Migraine Trust
45 Great Ormond Street
London WC1N 3HD
0171-831 4818

Miscarriage Association
c/o Clayton Hospital
Northgate
Wakefield
West Yorkshire WF4 4TP
01924 200799

Myalgic Encephalomyelitis Association
Mrs Maris Moore
Stanhope House
High Street
Stanford-le-Hope
Essex SS17 0HA
01375 642466

Relate
Herbert Gray College
Little Church Street
Rugby
Warwickshire CV21 3AP
01788 573241

Phobics' Society
26 Kensington Road
Chorlton cum Hardy
Manchester M21 9QJ
0161-881 1937

British Association of Psychotherapists
37 Mapesbury Road
London NW2 4HJ
0181-452 9823
Training institute with 400 psychotherapists on their books

Psycho-Analytical Society
63 New Cavendish Street
London W1M 7RD

Society of Analytical Psychology
1 Daleham Gardens
London NW3 5BY
0171-435 7696

Samaritans
17 Uxbridge Road
Slough
Berkshire SL1 1SN
01753 531011
Local branches throughout the country

As well as numerous other organisations and self-help groups which you can approach, it is important to remember that your GP can refer you directly to a clinical psychologist, through the National Health Service. Even if this does not provide the counselling you need, a psychologist may help you to know where to turn for help.

Index